Transformational Leadership

Empowering the Church
Transforming the Nations

by Dr. Kwame Gilbert

Copyright © 2012 by Dr. Kwame Gilbert

Transformational Leadership
by Dr. Kwame Gilbert

Printed in the United States of America

ISBN 9781619964228

All rights reserved solely by the author. The author guarantees all contents are original and do not infringe upon the legal rights of any other person or work. No part of this book may be reproduced in any form without the permission of the author. The views expressed in this book are not necessarily those of the publisher.

Unless otherwise indicated, Bible quotations are taken from the King James Version. Copyright © 1979 by Thomas Nelson.

www.xulonpress.com

Table of Contents

Foreword 9

INTRODUCTION 11

CHAPTER 1
A World in Crisis: a secular Mindset
vs. a Biblical Response 15

CHAPTER 2
Leadership versus Management..30

CHAPTER 3
The Church: Both Organism and Organization 48

CHAPTER 4
The Church: Its Mission, Message,
and Messenger 62

CHAPTER 5
Profile of a successful Leader 82

CHAPTER 6
To Be Salt and Light 101

CHAPTER 7
The Cost of Leadership 122

CHAPTER 8
A Transformed Leader: Transformed Nation 135

Dedication

I give glory and honor to my Lord and savior Jesus Christ, for his love and mercy, of which I am undeserving. He has been my constant friend and without him I am truly nothing. I give thanks to him and to the many wonderful people he has brought into my life that have in one way or another contributed to my completion of this book.

To my World Vision family, thank you for standing by me through the birthing pangs, and growing pains of our journey together. You are a great church. To my faithful friends and brothers in ministry, thank you all for inspiring me, and believing in me when I was bombarded by hell, and many times felt like giving up. Your words of encouragement have always been a lifter of my soul. May you receive a harvest of souls.

To my parents: Thelma my mother, you have always been afraid for me and the risks I take. Fear not my mother, my trust is not in the arm of flesh. Reuben my Dad, your wisdom has always been a secret weapon and your life of prayer; an enduring legacy. To my brothers and sisters, thank you for your unwavering love and support.

I dedicate this book to my beloved wife Rona, for lovingly, patiently, faithfully holding the fabric of our family together over these many years of my studies, ministry, political engagement, and now the completion of this book. Thank you and I forever love you. To my sons Jered and Edrei, for the joy and pride you give me in being your dad.

Foreword

This erudite, eloquent, and immensely thought-provoking work gets to the heart of the deepest passions and aspirations of the human heart - the search for True leadership.

This is indispensable reading for anyone who wants to live life above the norm. This is a profound authoritative work which spans the wisdom of the ages and yet breaks new ground in its approach and will possibly become a classic in this and the next generation.

This exceptional work by Kwame is one of the most profound, practical, principle-centered approaches to the subject on Leadership I have read in a long time. The author's approach to this timely and critical issue of leadership brings a fresh breath of air that captivates the heart, engages the mind and inspires the spirit of the reader.

The author's ability to leap over complicated theological and metaphysical jargon and reduce complex theories to simple practical leadership principles that the least among us can understand is amazing.

This work will challenge the intellectual while embracing the laymen as it dismantles the mysterious of the soul search of mankind and delivers the profound in simplicity.

Kwame's approach awakens in the reader the untapped inhibiters that retard our personal leadership development and his antidotes empower us to rise above these self-defeating, self-limiting factors to a life of exploits in spiritual and mental advancement.

The author also integrates into each chapter the time-tested precepts giving each principle a practical application to life making the entire process people-friendly.

Every sentence of this book is pregnant with wisdom and I enjoyed the mind-expanding experience of this exciting book. I admonish you to plunge into this ocean of knowledge and watch your life change for the better as you experience Transformational leadership.

Dr. Myles Munroe
BFM International
ITWLA
Nassau Bahamas

Introduction

It was July 21, 2006, at about two pm when my mobile phone rang. The female voice on the line identified herself as the secretary of the President of Guyana and informed me that His Excellency the President was seeking to have an audience with me at my earliest convenience. I quickly recovered from my surprise, donned a very businesslike tone to my voice, and informed her that I will make myself available within a few hours.

The ensuing meeting with the President began a chapter in my life which has brought me into an engagement in public life, serving within the hierarchy of national government. I must hasten to add that such an assignment has not come without great personal cost and great pain. It is out of this pain of being vilified, misrepresented and alienated by the very community that I love and serve, that has birthed this discourse which I now begin. This book seeks to address some of the misunderstandings and misinterpretations existing in the Christian community regarding the church and its involvement in national issues. It answers the question, what do we do with our professionals in our churches? Should Christians be involved in the politics of their country? It seems to me that a lot of the preaching we have heard has suggested that God wants to and can only

use the unlearned. For those who have had the 'misfortune' of higher learning and education, 'sorry, God does not need your degree'! Well, I respectfully insist that in this time of apostolic realignment, there is a place for both the unlearned and the PhDs in advancing the Kingdom of God in the earth. The truth is that our ability, accomplishments or titles is not what gives success in spiritual things. It is our submission and availability to God.

My decision to engage in the process of nation building through a political appointment was considered by many within the Christian community as a betrayal and an abandonment of my faith. Many ill things were said about me in private meetings while others publicly vilified me from their pulpits and on their radio and television programs. Was I hurt? Absolutely! It is a painful experience to suffer the loss of relationships, particularly those within the community of believers. Part of the problem for the church, I realized, was the internal conflict of the call to be separated from the world, but at the same time advance the kingdom of God within the very world systems we are called to oppose. It is this anomaly that caused many of my friends and colleagues to straddle the fence of indecision and confusion regarding Christian political involvement.

The nature of Guyana's politics is extremely divisive, and heavily polarized along racial lines. We also do have a very bitter and painful history, from which we as a nation have not yet recovered. Involvement in politics therefore is an extremely risky undertaking, and for a Christian minister, it can be considered almost suicidal. My decision therefore to be involved is not borne by any selfish or personal desire for fame or wealth. I have been blessed with a congregation who looks out for my interest, and my opportunities to travel the world in the preaching of the gospel are many. My decision therefore to become involved in politics is rooted in the biblical mandate to be the Salt and the Light of the World, and the indisputable fact that I have a covenantal responsibility for the destiny of my nation.

Hosea reminds us in Chapter 4 verse 6 that "my people are destroyed for a lack of knowledge, because thou has rejected knowledge, I will also reject thee..." We are also admonished in Proverbs 19:2 that "the soul without knowledge is not good...." My prayer is that as we consider together the transformational leadership principles for the empowering of the church and the transformation of nations, that your vision for your life, ministry and nation will be crystallized and captured, and you will never be the same again.

Chapter 1

A World in Crisis: a secular Mindset vs. a Biblical Response

Anyone who has lived on this planet during the past forty years, and has experienced the kinds of changes in our physical environments, social institutions and economies, would be justified in their conclusion that our world is in a crisis. Arguably, we have seen phenomenal technological advancements in many areas, which are of great benefit to the human race. But it requires no special intellectual or scientific capability to make simple comparisons between where we were and where we are now, in some very important areas of human development. There are observable changes taking place every day; changes that are redefining some very basic and fundamental laws and principles that govern our planet.

Change is inevitable. From creation to now, the world has gone through so many changes that sometimes it is hard to even remember how things used to be. At times I try to recall how life was, before mobile phones. It seems inconceivable that there was ever a time that we did not have these modern conveniences, although some friends of mine would prefer to call them necessities. But the truth is, there was a time when we did not have them, yet we were able to conduct the affairs of our lives with some degree of order and stability. These days, if I do forget my mobile at home for half of a day, I get the feeling that the world has moved on for that half of a day, and I have to catch up. All around us, change is taking place; some in a controlled, manageable environment, which leads to innovation and development, and others, in environments that are volatile, unstable, and even diabolically engineered. But the thing about change is that it has to be managed, if it will be of any benefit. It is unmanaged change which results in the crisis to which I allude. The signs are everywhere: Our planet may very well be in a crisis.

We often get stuck on the description of our problems and scarcely move to a prescriptive solution. It is my considered view, that change can be used for good, if it is properly understood. Most of us are rather afraid of change, because it threatens our modality of security and stability. Our aversion to change can actually work against us, if that aversion is driven by fear of the unknown or the unproven. While I do consider tradition to be of great value in the preservation of time honored norms and cultural values, tradition if taken too far, can actually become an enemy of creativity and ingenuity. The response therefore to change, must first be that we seek to understand change, and then, change as the changes dictate.

Now it may seem like a rather unbiblical thing to ask, particularly for those of us who are conservatives, and one can understand the initial trepidation. The question I assume that pops into your mind is, "Aren't Christians called to swim against the tide? Aren't we to stand tall in defiance to any form of unscriptural or unholy compromises?" So why should we seek to conform to external changes? Permit me to briefly clarify what is being suggested.

For example, we have been taught since first grade that long before man came into being, dinosaurs walked on our planet. Well, forgive me for not wasting your time in seeking to prove or disprove this theory. I think we both agree that this is not the purpose of this material. But just for the sake of argument, let's agree that big old dinosaurs did walk on our planet. They tell us that dinosaurs lived some two hundred and thirty million years ago. The explanation offered for the extinction of these prehistoric creatures, is that over time, the climatic conditions in which these animals existed began to change. The weather affected the vegetation, and consequently, the natural habitat of these creatures began to change. The dinosaurs, being unable to change in consonance with the environment began to die and eventually became extinct. The implication therefore is that every day, changes are taking place all around us. Unless we seek to understand these changes and make the necessary adjustments to ensure we remain relevant and effective, we the "Christian breed" can find ourselves becoming an extinct irrelevant, ineffective breed of people.

Environmental Changes

Experts have told us that the temperature of the earth has been on the increase during the 20th century. This increase in the earth's temperature is more familiarly called global warming. It is allegedly responsible for a continuous rise in sea levels around the world. Consequently, they surmise, floods, hurricanes and tornadoes are coming at us with alarming rapidity. Countries such as Guyana, that are heavily dependent on a stable weather pattern for its agricultural sustainability, are finding it very difficult to sustain their economies in the face of these challenges. Evidence of this is seen in the report of the assessment conducted by the United Nations Economic Commission for Latin America and The Caribbean (ECLAC) estimates for Guyana. A recent National Geographic article sums it up this way.

"The Planet is warming, from North Pole to South Pole, and everywhere in between. Globally, the mercury is already up more than 1 degree Fahrenheit (0.8 degree Celsius) and even more in sensitive Polar Regions. And the effects of rising temperatures aren't waiting for some far –flung future. They're happening right now. Signs are appearing all over, and some of them are surprising. The heat is not only melting glaciers and sea ice; it's also shifting precipitation patterns and setting animals on the move."

If one is to accept the initial research regarding the effects of global warming, they range from earthquakes from as far as China, to Haiti; avalanches, volcanoes in Iceland, floods, tsunamis and wildfires. We live in a World that's in crisis.

Economic Crisis

The World's economy tottered dangerously on the brink of an economic collapse between 2007 and 2009. The first few months of 2010 did show encouraging signs of a reversal of fortunes which may or may not continue into 2011. I hold no great familiarity with the subject of economics, but from a layman's perspective, the financial crisis that almost brought the world to its knees, occurred due to what recent research has shown to be questionable financial practices by decision makers in many of our leading financial institutions. One wrong action, or maybe a series of them, led to multiplied chain reactions throughout the financial sectors of the World's economy. Many of the financial pundits of this century proclaimed that they have not seen the likes of this crisis, since the Great Depression of the nineteen thirties. Alan Greenspan the former Federal Reserve chairman of the US said "The current financial crisis in the US is likely to be judged as the most wrenching since the end of the Second World War." It was also posited by billionaire investor George Soros that "The collapse of the financial system as we know it is real, and the crisis is far from over." Naturally, when the blame shifting began, the list of names of corporations and individuals found culpable grew by the minute. One thing was very clear to me as I viewed the unfolding saga. The world is in crisis, and it will become increasingly worse where greed and ostentation is rampant, and in the absence of bible- based leadership.

Deterioration of the family

It would appear from casual observation that there seem to be an evolution in how the institution of family is now organized and regarded. This so-called evolution, embraces the doctrines of individualism, and relativism. We see for example in the context of marital relationships a contradiction in the co-dependence of a husband and wife on each other. It rejects the absoluteness of the word of God, as the standard by which the family must be constituted. It further encourages women to seek after and assert their individuality and independence outside of a covenant relationship with a husband. I am not opposed to the independence of women at all. In fact I am of the firm view that women should be given every opportunity to develop themselves and maximize every God given ability and potential they possess. What I am concerned about however, is the extreme to which some individuals will go in seeking to invalidate the value and sacredness of the institutions of marriage and family. The family is considered to be the most basic or central of all human institutions. Its success or failure therefore, will inevitably have impact on every other human institution. It is in the family that children are raised and socialized, hence determining their functions in the wider society. It is interesting to note that doctors, teachers, and pastors, as well as rapists and murderers are also raised in families. What are the factors that contribute to how one family raises a well-adjusted, productive individual, while another raises an individual who becomes a liability to society?

Dr. Godfrey St. Bernard of the University of the West Indies, in his scholarly presentation entitled *Major trends affecting families in Central America and the Caribbean,* identified a number of contributors to the decline in family. Interestingly, St. Bernard cites the prevalence of female headed households, and the absence of male authority figures as two of the major contributors to the crisis in the family. He further points out that "eighty-three percent (83%) of the children born into the Jamaican society are born to single women. Approximately twenty percent of all births each year are to mothers nineteen years and younger. St. Bernard went on to say:

> " It is generally acknowledged, particularly in developed societies, that children in homes in which the father is absent tend to manifest anti-social behavior, delinquency, depression, early sexual initiation, drug abuse, low academic performance, higher school dropout rates which all culminate in later years into low career attainment and low productivity on a national level."

From a sociological perspective, the family is in a crisis. From a Biblical perspective the family is also in crisis. The Scripture gives us clear directives regarding how God intends for the family to function. In Deuteronomy 6:-8; Proverbs 10: 1, 5, and Ephesians 6: 1, 2 and 4, we see that God intended the family be the primary place of social interaction. Sadly this is far removed from our present reality. Many families today briefly see each other as they rush through the kitchen and hallways, on their way out to another job or social activity. Sunday evening dinners with the entire family around the dinner table are a thing of the past. Family devotions and family worship is missing from many homes. In some homes, Christian homes at that, the only spiritual activity shared by the family, is the weekly visits to the house of God. Play time is replaced by endless, silent hours in front of the television. I am convinced, and mounting evidence confirms, that the family, both Christian and non-Christian, is in a crisis.

Political Tensions

Our daily news is inundated with stories of continuing and emerging political tensions around the Globe. From Hong Kong to Bangkok, and from Pakistan to Kenya, tensions are rising and the United Nations and its resources are stretched thin to keep up with increasing pressures to bring resolution to these conflicts. The winds of war continue to blow in the Middle East, and lives are being lost every day in Afghanistan. The truth remains; our world is in a crisis.

A Secular Mindset vs. a Biblical Response

When one considers the nature of the crises we are in, it becomes clear that at the root of most of our problems is the issue of leadership. There is no crisis I can think of that is not somehow linked to a breakdown or failure of leadership. Let us consider the social problems that I enumerated earlier. The increase of global temperature, it is believed, has been brought on by a combination of factors. Experts have explained that it is primarily the release of greenhouse gases into the atmosphere, and the consequential damage of the protective ozone layer, which contributes to this phenomenon. It is widely believed by the leading environmentalists that climate change is the result of irresponsible, environmentally unfriendly government policies. In 1988, the Intergovernmental Panel on Climate Change (IPCC) was created by the United Nations Environment Program (UNEP) and the World Meteorological Organization (WMO) to assess the scientific knowledge on global warming. The IPCC concluded in 1990 that there was broad international consensus that climate change was human-induced. I stand by my argument therefore, that the crisis we face is as a result of failed leadership. In the context of climate change, I contend that if the governments of the developed, industrialized countries had embraced a more responsible posture to the environment and the preservation of the planet, the crisis with which we are now faced in relation to the overheating of our planet, could have been averted. Of course it becomes necessary to consider that in less regulated countries such as China and India, the pressures of providing the basic necessities of its people, may reduce this issue to being secondary in importance. Its implications however must not be ignored.

The question I am sure you must be asking is: What has global warming got to do with leadership? My response is: everything. In the book of Genesis, chapter 1 verse 26, God established an authority structure which he intended to be the model of governance for the earth. In verse twenty six, God decreed "Let us make man in our image, after our likeness and let them, have dominion over the fish of the sea and over the fowl of the air, and over the cattle and over every creeping thing that creeps upon the earth." (KJV). Secondly, in chapter 2 verse 15, God placed man in the garden with a specific mandate to, "Dress it and to keep it." There are two things in these passages which help us to understand why we are in the plight we are in today. First, when God said, "let them have dominion," he was consigning the responsibilities for the management of the earth and all of its affairs into the hands of man. In other words, in this text, God was giving to man the responsibility to lead and take charge of his environment. The environmental crisis that we are now faced with may very well be as a result of man's sad abdication of his responsibility to lead and take charge of his environment. Instead of recognizing this, we have sought to levy blame at every possible level for what is happening to our planet. I contend, and strongly so, that a return of our leaders to an understanding and embracing of the biblical mandate of "dressing and keeping" of the garden (earth) will see a manifestation of environmental transformation. It must be noted also that the fall of man through the advent of sin, did remove from man this ability to exercise dominion. Hence in order for man to accomplish this, he must also be free of the sin nature.

The crisis in our economies is also with no doubt, a crisis of leadership. The absence of regulations and guidelines will unavoidably give rise to excesses and ostentation. Why? This is so, because the hearts of men are deceitful, and from creation to now, we are still driven to sin by "the lust of the eye, the lust of the flesh and the pride of life."(1 Jn. 2:16) Men, who are not transformed by the power of the Holy Spirit, are unrelentingly driven by greed and covetousness. It is this cruel taskmaster that possessed the hearts of some, which drove them to conceive Ponzi schemes and violate codes of ethics and financial propriety. What is at the root of this? Again I insist; a crisis of leadership. This crisis begins at the personal level and escalates to the governmental levels.

When we speak of government, people automatically begin to think of civil government. But there is a level of government which we talk very little about these days. McDowell & Beliles in their writing, *Liberating the Nations,* speak of a concept of "self-government." The argument is proffered that, "the type of government that exists in the home, churches, schools, businesses, associations, or civil realms, of a country is a reflection of the self-government within the citizen." 1Timothy 3; 4-5 sets out clearly, that for a man to lead others he must first lead himself. In this specific context, it speaks to church leaders, but the principle is applicable to all spheres of leadership. Here is what it says: "...the leader must manage his own household well, keeping his children under control with all dignity. But if a man does not know how to manage his own household, how will he take care of the church of God?" (I Timothy 3:4-5) The same self- government principle is set forth in the book of Proverbs. He who is slow to anger is better than the mighty, and he who rules his spirit, than he who captures a city." (Proverbs 16:32). The Global economic crisis, it can be argued, may very well be the result of men who have failed in self-government which is a reflection of a crisis in leadership. I would argue that as the man is, so is the family. As is the family, so is the society. It is clear therefore, that people who have been entrusted with the responsibility of financial leadership of a country, but who instead seek to pursue their own narrow and selfish interest, are really individuals who have failed in the government of their own lives. As is the society, so is the government. A man, who leads his own life well, will inevitably lead a bank or a nation well.

The crisis in the family is indisputably a crisis of leadership. When fathers are either physically or emotionally absent from the home, it leaves the home susceptible to the influences of the surrounding cultures and robs it of that divine covering that comes from a man being in that covenant place where God has placed him.

It is rather alarming that the response to all of these crises facing our planet, all seem to ignore the real root cause of the problems. Many social theorists have sought to provide all sorts of scientific and empirical arguments as to what is responsible for the crisis facing the family. Some, such as Paul Vitz, argue that "it is apparent that by far the single most important factor in the many social problems presently confronting us is the failure of fathers, the fact that men have abandoned their role in the family"

From a biblical perspective, we can easily identify some of the standards which have been set as pillars of a healthy and successful family. It is the continuous violation and disregard for these principles which have inevitably led to many of the broken homes we see today. But the question that begs to be answered is: what is the relationship between leadership and the crisis within the family, the economy, or in the nation?

The dominion mandate given to Adam in Genesis was not nullified on the basis of his transgression. It is still God's desire that man exercise dominion over the earth as he originally intended for Adam. Adam was created with the innate ability to administer over the affairs of the earth, as God's power of attorney. Consider that when God mandated Adam to name the animals, God had no need to bring correction to anything Adam did. Whatever Adam called it that is what it is today. This to my mind speaks of a divine capability which God had placed in Adam, in order that he might represent God in the Earth. It is through the advent of sin that Adam and consequently, mankind, lost that divine ability to effectively administer the affairs of our Creator in the earth. In essence, Adam could no longer lead as God intended for him to lead. Sin, robbed man of his God ordained place of authority and dominion. The present state of our planet is as a consequence of man's loss of his place of leadership. The world consequently was thrown into a state of disarray. The socio-political disequilibrium that we are presently experiencing is reflective of this lost of divine management.

With regards to all said so far, we see in our present day realities evidence which would suggest that the affairs of our world are now being controlled by a satanic regime. The divine intention of God now seems to be subverted by a heathen, atheistic culture that violates everything that represents God. In essence, sin disqualified man from exercising leadership over the earth. But the good news is that through the redemptive work of Christ, mankind is now repositioned to take up his place of management of the earth. Jesus told his disciples that they now had power to legislate both in the affairs of heaven and earth, when he announced in Matthew 16:19, "And I will give unto thee the keys to the kingdom of heaven: and whatsoever thou shall bind on earth shall be bound in heaven: and whatsoever thou shall loose on earth shall be loosed in heaven." (KJV).

It is clear therefore that in Christ, the dominion mandate is restored to the redeemed; the sons of God. The response therefore to all that is happening has to be one that is based on biblical principles. Men and women of God, who possess a sense of destiny with an understanding of the principles of the kingdom, must now more than ever before, begin to engage their world. Leadership based on biblical principles is the solution to the needs of this hour. The planet is not without hope. Our homes, our families, our communities our nation, are not without remedy. The Bible provides the solution, the answer to the crisis of our time. What this world needs is for the sons of God, the redeemed, to rise up and take dominion of the earth. The Church, the blood-washed, followers of Christ, empowered and engaged, is the solution to this crisis.

Chapter 2

Leadership versus Management

A need for leadership

Leafing through a history book, one comes across the names of many people who have made profound imprints on societal life. There are great men and women who have started revolutionary movements that changed human history. There is no doubt that outstanding personalities play an important role in history. For instance, one cannot deny the great contribution of Mahatma Gandhi to India's history. But where did his strengths lie? A close examination of his life would reveal that Gandhi expressed in his life and labors, the interest of the masses in a movement of the Indian people against colonialism. That was why the people elected and supported him as their leader.

Admittedly, there were many progressive intellectuals in India before Gandhi, who opposed the British oppressors. Many of them were persecuted, imprisoned and deported. The Indian people regarded them as national heroes. But none of them came close to receiving the love and support that the people gave to Gandhi. Why? Gandhi was in touch with the people and they weren't. The efforts of outstanding individuals will always fail, regardless of how well intentioned, if they are out of touch with the people: if they do not express the urgent requirement of social development.

Let us consider what would have become of history if, for instance, Martin Luther King had died in his childhood or had never been born. Not only he, but consider the fathers of our nations as well, who fought and endured much, for the liberties we now enjoy. Hence, we must concur that outstanding personalities play an important role in history.

A study of the outstanding personalities of different epochs will show that the historical importance of their activities has always been determined by the scope of the social movement they represent. I contend that it is the cause that the leader represents that gives him his following. Recently, a close friend of mine, who is of another ethnic origin, said to me "Reverend, as a friend to a friend, there is a crisis of leadership in the black community."

At first admittedly, I was offended and began to object vehemently, since the inference of what he said could be misinterpreted. Then as I gave deeper consideration to his perspective, I concurred. You see, he did not say a crisis of managers, politicians or businessmen. He said the crisis is in "leadership". As I examine the political environment in Guyana, I would want to further suggest that it is possible that this crisis is not endemic to my ethnic community only but to the whole nation. The word leadership is from the Greek verb proistemi, which describes the position of a seaman who stands on the bow in front of the others to point out the destination and ways and means of reaching the port. He sets direction and inspires others to follow. He is a people's person whose focus is to influence people to a particular course of action. Because he is people oriented, his power is influenced to move people to act. This influence stems from shared vision, personal integrity, and the ability to foster collations among people.

So let us consider my friend's observation against my definition of leadership, in the context of a socio-political matrix. Do we have leaders within our community, political, religious and otherwise, who are committed to service first to the people? The dilemma we are faced with is that some who are esteemed as leaders within our communities both political and religious, sometimes use their influence to destroy rather than to build. Those of us who are aspiring for political office need to ask ourselves a few necessary questions. Is social development and adding value to the lives of our people the ultimate motivation, or is it that we are driven by personal pride or a hunger for power? As we examine the political landscape of the nations of the earth, do we see leaders who are willing to sacrifice their political ambitions in the interest of the people they have been elected to serve? What about personal integrity? Do we as leaders, both in the religious and political context, live out in our private lives what we preach in public?

Great political movements triumph not because of the groundswell of the majority, but because people have found leaders that they are willing to die for, who embrace a cause that he or she is willing to die for. We have no short supply of managers, what we desperately need are more leaders.

In light of the aforementioned, comparison must be drawn between a leader and a manager, recognizing that the two are not necessarily the same. A leader should be a good manager but it does not necessarily follow, that a manager is a leader. It would be useful to note as well that many leaders who have shaped history were themselves not very good managers, but in understanding their limitations, surrounded themselves with people who were adept at managing. Leadership and management share many similarities. Both leadership and management involve influence, working with people, and working with effective goal management. However, the fields of leadership and management can also be considered very different. According to John Kotter, leadership can be considered an age-old concept that has been around for centuries, while management is a concept developed in the last 100 years, in part from the rise of the industrial revolution.

In speaking of the leadership crisis in the world, Robert A. Orr said, " We look nice and orderly on paper but the truth is that so many of our organizations are static and going nowhere because of the lack of leadership and good management, coupled with a lack of good and proper communication."

Management in the secular context refers to an employee who is charged with making decisions, leading people, and delegating authority in order to accomplish the goals of the organization. A manager is generally responsible for recognizing and recommending rewards for achievement. It is clear from this definition, that there are a number of functional responsibilities that determines the parameters and influence of the manager. The element of decision making recognizes that the manager is tasked with the assimilation and analyzing of relevant information, which guides him or her in making decisions or coming to conclusions regarding the strategic direction of the organization. While the definition also recognizes the manager to be someone who leads people, it is not necessarily true that all managers possess the core competency of people -skills required to lead people. Additionally, some managers may not necessarily have within their assignment the task of leading people as a significant part of their job responsibilities, especially in cases where the operation is heavily mechanized. Hence a manager may be a good manager based on his specific job responsibilities, but may not be an effective leader of people.

The famous quote by Peter Drucker gives us a different perspective on management as well, when he pointed out that, "so much of what we call management consists of making it difficult for people to work." The common denominator in the principles of management and leadership is that both have to deal with people. It may be that a manager has a greater focus on achieving organizational goals rather than on people development, therefore the emphasis or focus of these two individuals may of necessity vary, based on the motivation. It could also be that based on the fact that managers are appointed but leaders emerge in times of need or crisis, the manager will therefore seek to do that which secures returns or rewards, while the leader does that which secures the well being of those he leads.

In a famous Drucker quote the point is made that "leadership is doing the right thing and management is doing things right." This illustrates how the two skill sets need to work together. In order to be fully rounded, a leader must have the ability to manage the day to day tasks and deliver results, while seeing the big picture and the opportunity for change.

Demonstrating good leadership skills without the management skills to support it will leave you with an inability to really put even the best of visions together and implement effectively. Likewise, being a good manager without good leadership skills will cause continual challenges in motivating the team and producing the results he or she is seeking to accomplish. Being able to blend leadership and management is truly a unique skill set. Keep in mind, there is an abundance of managers in the world but very few truly embody the characteristics of a leader. It can also be argued that leaders do not have subordinates - at least not when they are leading. Many organizational leaders do have subordinates, but only because they are also managers. But when they want to lead, they have to give up formal authoritarian control, because to lead is to have followers, and following is always a voluntary activity.

It was Kenneth Blanchard who said, "The key to successful leadership today is influence not authority."

Toor & Ofori, in discussing management and leadership and their differences, posit that these are two entirely different functions based on their underlying philosophies, functions, and outcomes. Similarly, leaders and managers are not the same people. They apply different conceptualizations and approaches to work, exercise different ways of problem solving, undertake different functions in the organization, and exhibit different behaviors owing to their different intrinsic and extrinsic motivations. Although discretely different, the terms "manager" and "leader" are often confused and used interchangeably. But who is a manager, and who is a leader? Leslie Kossoff argues that, "The difference between being a manager and being a leader is simple. Management is a career. Leadership is a calling."

To fully appreciate this view expressed by Kossoff we must examine the fundamental characteristics of managers and leaders. As was earlier discussed, leadership is just one of the many qualities a successful manager must possess. Care must be taken in distinguishing between the two concepts. The main aim of a manager is to maximize the output of the organization through administrative implementation. To achieve this, managers must undertake the following functions: organization, planning, staffing, directing, and controlling.

A manager cannot just be a leader; he also needs formal authority to be effective. It is argued by Daniel Predpall that, "for any quality initiative to take hold, senior management must be involved and act as a role model. This involvement cannot be delegated." A leader on the other hand, is someone who people naturally follow through their own choice, whereas a manager must be obeyed. A manager may only have obtained his position of authority through time and loyalty given to the organization, not as a result of his leadership qualities. A leader may have no organizational skills, but his vision unites people behind him. It is further contended by Daniel Predpall that, "Leaders must let vision, strategies, goals, and values be the guide-post for action and behavior rather than attempting to control others."

When considering the concept of leadership, one cannot do so effectively without giving recognition to the model of leadership held out by scripture, and exemplified by the greatest leader who lived- Jesus Christ himself. It is posited by Wilkes that, " many churches struggle because they lack servant leaders" Indeed , as one considers the present culture of today's church , one would observe that what is held out by scripture as a model of servant leadership , is not so readily practiced in churches today. In referring to Jesus' approach to leadership, Mark reminds us, "for even the Son of Man did not come to be served, but to serve, and give his life as a ransom for many" (Mark 10:45, NIV). This model of leadership was indeed modeled rather effectively by Jesus, who we see consistently in scripture demonstrating the attitude of service to his disciples as well as to those who came to him seeking help in their difficulties. We see him demonstrating his servant leadership in John 13: 5, by washing the feet of his disciples, as an object lesson to them of the need to serve each other in humility. It was J. Oswald Sanders who said, "True greatness, true leadership, is achieved not by reducing men to one's service but in giving oneself in selfless service to them."

In teaching the early Christians at Philippi about the Christ like attitudes, Paul the Apostle encourages this group of early believers to serve each other in the same way that Jesus would serve them. He reminds them that the source of their strength, fellowship and unity, was in their relationship with Christ (Philippians 2:5-11). This raises a very important consideration. It would be safe to conclude based on Paul's admonition, that the ability to manifest a servant type leadership, is dependent on one's relationship with Christ. Now in closer examination of verse 8 of the chapter, Paul referred to Jesus as "humbling himself", setting forth as a vital characteristic of servant leadership, the virtue of humility. The distinguishing characteristic of a leader in the Church of Jesus Christ today therefore must not be his intellectual acumen or managerial skills, but his servant- hood. It is aptly put by Calvin Miller who said, "The number one quality that must mark tomorrow's leaders is servant hood."

Earlier I made reference to the instance of Jesus washing the feet of his disciples as a demonstration of servant leadership. I want to insist that Jesus was also modeling another valuable principle before his disciples. Washing their feet was not his job or his duty. He was their master, their Lord. But he did this to demonstrate that leaders meet needs. Consider that all of the disciples in that room had feet that were dirty, but none of them made any attempts to meet another's need. Jesus did, and set for us a powerful principle. That principle is that leaders look for, and meet needs.

Another important principle we see in this story in John 13: 4 to 11, is that Jesus did not discriminate in his service. He washed the feet of even the very one who would later betray him. This is indeed a true manifestation of kingdom leadership in action.

Leadership is not characterized only by servant-hood. Kenneth Gangel in discussing the meaning of leadership articulates that leadership is also stewardship. A good example of this concept of stewardship in leadership is seen in the parable of the faithful and wise manager who was placed in charge of other servants not to lord it over them but to ensure that their basic provisions were taken care of.(Luke 12: 42-46).

In recent times, secular literature has discussed a great deal about shared power and empowerment of people. The evidence shows however, that this is not a principle widely practiced by secular society. In fact, what seem to be the approach is a self centered, desperate, retaining of power. Get power and hold on to it, no matter the cost. Incidentally this seems to be the attitude of some, both in religious leadership as well as the political arenas. The pattern of empowerment of others and the sharing of power is a biblical one as is evidenced in Philippians 2:14 which instruct that, "Christian leaders serve not their own interest but rather the interest of others." It is instructive to note that this biblical model has been responsible for significant success in many groups and organization, working in team efforts. What is evident in this model is the absence of individualism and isolation. In such instances, individuals as well as the collective process benefit from contributions to not only the common agenda, but also individuals which ultimately empower the team. The practice which is evident in more progressive organizations, and which is also recommended for maximum results, is that of devolution of power within the organization. This would allow for decision making to take place at the lower levels and not necessarily only at the top management levels as is the case in the hierarchical management structures. New Testament patterns of leadership, emphasizes the need for modeling of behavior as a key element of biblical leadership. We see evidence in 1 Timothy 4: 11 to 16 of Paul admonishing Timothy, a younger man to set an example; model a certain kind of behavior, which Paul himself modeled quite effectively as well, before Timothy his protégé. Richards &Hoeldtke sum up this principle by saying, "The spiritual leader who is a servant does not demand. He serves. In his service the spiritual leader sets an example for the body; an example that has compelling power to motivate heart change."

A discussion on leadership and management would be incomplete if consideration is not given to the issue of bad leadership and mismanagement. Leroy Eims in his writing *Be the Leader You were Meant to Be*, states that; " political leaders, economic experts, editorial writers, news people, spokespeople in areas such as education and religion are searching for people who know the way and can lead others on the right path- a crisis of leadership engulfs the world." Eims is spot on target in his conclusion. There is definitely a crisis of leadership, and more particularly, bible based leadership.

We are given some useful insights into the nature of leadership in Matthew 9: 36-38 where three basic elements of leadership are discussed. First, we can conclude from this text, that leadership is a God-given capacity and responsibility, to influence a specific group of God's people in pursuit of God's purpose for that group. The leader must have the capacity that empowers him or her to be able to convert great intentions into achievable realities that are sustainable. The ability of the leader is also manifested in how he is able to influence his followers into action and make them agents of change. It must be noted that the "God-givenness" of leadership capacity or ability stands out clearly. When one gives consideration to this it is recognized that leaders cannot just be made. From a Christian perspective on spiritual gifts, this is an accurate view. While it is true that as believers we can desire spiritual gifts, we must be reminded that it is God who gives gifts to us. Because a leader is people-oriented, his power is seen in his influence to move people to act.

This influence stems from a shared vision, personal integrity, and the ability to foster coalitions among people.

Stephen Covey, in Principle-Centered Leadership, discusses the fundamental differences between leadership and management. He recognizes that, "leadership deals with direction, vision, effectiveness and results." Covey continues in his analysis and declares that management deals with establishing structures and systems to obtain the desired results. Management according to Covey focuses on efficiency, cost-benefit analyses, logistics, methods, procedures and policies. Conversely, leadership focuses on top line, where management focuses on bottom line. His summation concludes that while management derives its power from values and correct principles, management organizes resources to serve selected objectives to produce the bottom line.

Further research on this subject, considers the work also of Dr. J. Robert Clinton, *The Making of a Leader*. Clinton purports that there are six stages involved in the development of a successful leader. First he speaks of a sovereign foundation, which relates to the events of a leader's life that prepares him for leadership. It may be that these events are unrelated, painful experiences, but which eventually, like tapestry they form a pattern of beauty. These include family life, upbringing, education, or environment. One can see the providence of God, His divine interventions in every stage of the believer's life. Second, there is what is referred to as "inner-life growth." In the training process of a leader, Clinton points to three elements in this process. (a) The leader's ability to receive and understand the word of God, and the power to influence others to a common goal depends on one's ability to clarify and apply God's unchanging word to changing situations. Every Christian leader has what can be referred to as a "word-gift" that forms part of his gift-mix. Clinton points out that the primary ones are: teaching, prophecy, and exhortation, the secondary ones are: apostleship, evangelism, and pastor. The written and living Word of God is the basic foundation upon which successful Christian leaders stand. For all of us who have been involved in ministry we would know that it is the Word of God that develops inner convictions that become our working assumptions in dealing with life situations and ministry. (b) Obedience is a vital part of the leader's development. We see the example of Abraham, when he was called, "he obeyed by going out to a place which he was to receive for an inheritance; and he went out not knowing where he was going" (Heb. 11:8). It must be noted that Abraham's obedience was not based on understanding but on submission to God's authority. He acted in faith and claimed God's promises. The same can be said about Paul the Apostle. He obeyed God's command as well. I want to clarify that this is not a recommendation for blind obedience. Obedience is unto the Lord. Abraham's greatest test of obedience to God's word came when he willingly followed God's command to sacrifice his son Isaac. I am sure that there would be concurrence from all Christian leaders that the willingness to surrender what is yours to obey God's

Word is a difficult test, and it is one that will continue to come our way. (c) The integrity of the leader cannot be overstated. This refers to an adherence to a code of ethics, artistic or other values, (sincerity, honesty, transparency). Apart from character, ministry is only religious activity, or even worst, religious business. As Warren Wiersbe said, "No amount of reputation can substitute for character" I surmise therefore that Christian leaders must develop a ministry philosophy that simultaneously honors biblical leadership values, embraces the challenges of the times in which they live , and fits their unique gifts and personal development if they expect to be productive over a whole lifetime.

Second, Clinton speaks of the establishing of values. This simply refers to the work a leader performs to define the values of the organization that will provide the indispensable content of a culture. The values therefore must result in "the way things are done" in the organization. The values must influence the beliefs, the rites, the rituals, the symbols and even the metaphors used by the organization. Christian leaders must be very clear about the core of their values they add to others. Our values are the products of our beliefs that shape character. They must be grounded in the Word of God. They are built-in assumptions into all that we do.

Third is the determination of strategy. This speaks of the work a leader performs to identify the crucial, critical objectives or activities necessary to achieve the corporate vision. Stephen Covey in Principle- Centered Leadership, pointed to a lack of strategic path in organization to achieve vision. It is posited that it is either that the strategy is not well developed or it ineffectively expresses the mission statement. It is not enough that the vision be clear, which in essence speaks to where the organization is going, but also that the strategy to get there is also clear. The Bible tells us that it is not enough to, "understand the times", but leaders must have, "knowledge of what Israel should do..." (1 Chron. 12:32).

Fourth is the responsibility to develop alignment. A crucial activity of leading is to align the whole organization to the vision. The negative effect would be everyone doing what is right in his own eyes. The Biblical injunction simply is that blessings come when two or three agree on things concerning God's will. It is not unusual for some organizations to be pulled in every which direction by dominant and influential parties. Hence God's leader must be vigilant in ensuring that the vision for that organization is clearly articulated and that the organization' strategies and plans are aligned with the corporate vision.

The fifth is the leaders mandate to motivate people. Perhaps one of the greatest challenges of leading is to make people want to work rather than just being made to work. In some of my earlier studies, I examined Maslows Hierarchy of Needs, which while it identifies levels of needs, does not work as a rigid series of steps where one is a requisite of the other. But people are motivated differently under different circumstances. For example, some people can be motivated by simply hearing a vision articulated clearly, because there is an intrinsic need that is being met in that vision. Others however are motivated to give their best because they are led by a leader that they emulate. A godly life is a great attraction and motivator. Of greater importance than the oratorical skills and great eloquence of the leader is a life of integrity which the leader lives out before his followers.

The sixth and final step is that of communication. Communication is the work of a leader to create understanding among people so that they can act effectively. This includes dissemination of organizational information such as corporate vision, policies, and programs to target audiences. People, to maintain a high level of commitment to the organization, are not satisfied in knowing what is done but also why it is being done. Many of the problems that I have encountered in my responsibility as a leader has to do with assumptions people have, because there is an absence of necessary information upon which to base a conclusion.

Even as the debate continues regarding the difference between leadership and management, recognition must be given to the fact that management is a tool that all leaders should have. In fact, the Christian leader in particular must employ management principles in his work if he will survive in the very demanding work of the ministry. Peter Drucker contends that because the pastor's job is mostly compassion, he needs to be able to manage in order to get the time, thought and freedom to get his work done. The church of Jesus today needs leaders. The world is crying out for more leaders and less managers. May we see an emerging of Godly men and women with courage to lead, possessing the skills and tools to manage.

Chapter 3

The Church: Both Organism and Organization

In beginning the discussion on the church as both an organism and organization, it would be useful to first of all examine the theological foundation of the church, and its development over the years. If there is ever a doctrinal or theological error which exist in today's Christian education, is the attempts often made by Christian teachers and preachers to compare the New Testament church with the Old Testament community of Israelites. It can often be heard in sermons that we as God's children are his "chosen people called to inherit a land of wealth and prosperity, flowing with milk and honey." While the scripture in 1 Peter 2:9 does say of the believer that we are a peculiar people , belonging to a royal priesthood, I believe that it is referring to a spiritual community, in pursuit of a spiritual kingdom and not a geographical plot of land somewhere . It is necessary to make the distinction therefore, that Israel was a nation of people that were the descendants of Abraham, singled out by God to be a special and peculiar people unto himself. Israel was a nation of people chosen by God through which he manifested his purposes. When God made His unconditional promise to Abraham that He would make his descendants a great nation, God also promised to bless all people through that nation (Genesis 12:1-3). Therefore, Israel was never considered a sole recipient of God's blessings, but rather, a channel for God's blessings to all mankind.

God's miracles for Israel, such as their dramatic deliverance from Egypt, were intended not only for the Israelites themselves, but as evidence of God's absolute power and uniqueness for a watching polytheistic world (Exodus 7:5; 14:18; Joshua 2:9-11). The Messiah that would come through the nation of Israel was always intended to be the Savior for all mankind (Isaiah 49:6). The Old Testament also contains many invitations to the entire world to come and worship the one living God in Israel (Psalm 2:10-12; 117:1). It is evident therefore that Israel as a nation had a special relationship with God in the specific context and time of the Old Testament.

The church on the other hand, is the ekklesia, which is the Greek word referring to an assembly of people summoned together. In the New Testament, the word ekklesia is translated "church" and speaks specifically of the congregation of God's people in Christ Jesus. In Eph. 2:19 it refers to those who are called together as citizens of God's Kingdom, coming together for the sole purpose of worshiping God. But the word "church" can also refer to the local church (Mat. 18:17), or it can mean the universal church (Acts 20:28). In this specific context, we are speaking of the local church, organized and functioning within a specific place or community.

There are several expressions used in scripture to describe the church. In 1 Corinthians, the church is referred to as the body of

Christ. This image indicates that no true church can really exists apart from vital union of the members with Christ. Our understanding therefore is that Christ is the Head of the Body and as the body, our sustenance and supply comes through that connection and relationship we share with him. The Church is a people with a future hope. This hope is rooted in the promise of the return of Christ to take his people with him. This "taking of God's people", is generally referred to as the Rapture, and several scriptures support the doctrine of this future hope (John 14:3, 1Tim. 6:14, Heb.9:28). The argument which I am therefore purporting is that the New Testament Church is not the same as the Old Testament community of Israelites.

The Church as an Organism

The Oxford dictionary defines an organism as "a system or organization consisting of interdependent parts, compared to a living being" . While there is no direct scriptural reference that labels the church as an organism, there are many scriptures which does recognize, based on the definition offered for an organism , that the church is an organism. Paul the Apostle in Romans 12: 5 records, "So in Christ we who are many form one body, and each member belongs to all the others". Additionally, in his writing to the church at Corinth he wrote: "For we were all baptized by one Spirit into one body" (1 Corinthians 12:13). These scriptures liken the church to a human body, thus confirming that it is indeed an organism.

In Col. 1:22 and 23, we see Paul painting a beautiful picture of the church as being the body of Christ. The intent, I believe is to communicate the idea of the church as a living, moving, breathing, organism, and not just an organization. The Church is a body comprising of people-men, women and children. It is a community of people who have put their trust and confidence in Jesus Christ for their salvation. We also see this image reflected in Ephesians 4:15 and 16:

> *....speaking the truth in a spirit of love, we [Christians] must grow up in every way to Christ, who is the head. Under His control all the different parts of the Body fit together, and the whole Body is held together by every joint with which it is provided So when each separate part works as it should, the whole body grows and builds itself up through love.*
>
> *There are a number of similarities between the physical body and the Body of Christ. While for example the toe and the ear have different locations and have different functions, they are still part of the same body. The eyes are able to detect danger in the path, while the feet guides and navigates the body, to avoid the danger. Both of which get their signals from the head (brain). Every*

member of the body therefore is essential to the proper working of the body.

This concept is also very true of the body of Christ. The anointed Pastor cannot say that he has no need of the traveling evangelist, or the talented worship leader. Neither can the Youth Leader say he can do well without the support of the counselor and the Sunday school superintendent. The Bank manager, who teaches the Sunday school class, is also as important as the elderly retired postman, who serves as the janitor of the local church. Both in their own way contribute to the health and development of the local church. Just as with the human body, there is diversity in this organism called the Church. All the different parts are fitted together, needing and supporting each other.

But it is not just diversity, but also unity that is manifested in this model. The human body houses the spirit of the person. The Body of Christ is the temple of the Holy Spirit. The presence of the Spirit in the believer draws each one together as members of the one Body of Christ. This unity means that what one part experiences have an effect on all other members of that Body.

If for example there is an injury to the leg, the whole rest of your body suffers along with it and seeks to help it. So also, the pain suffered by a mother who has lost her only child, also affects the older women who seek to minister to her also. In addition, the joy of one person coming to know Jesus Christ as Lord and Savior brings fulfillment to a believer who also has discovered the benefits of obeying Jesus Christ. Both the sadness and happiness of one member, has an impact on the rest of the Body of Christ.

Let us consider the issue of sin and discipline. What happens to the rest of the body when one member sins? As mentioned above in the case of the injured foot, one member's sin does affect the entire body. The story of Achan in Joshua chapter 7 comes to mind, where Achan's transgression caused Israel to lose not just a battle, but the lives of many valiant men. The sin of one member has grave implications for others in the body of Christ. But what are we to do with such a one? Are we to cut them off? Throw them out? Avoid association with them? In some Christian communities, the reaction to sin has been swift and decisive, ending with the erring brother or sister thrown out from amongst the "undefiled saints of God".

There is a part of the human anatomy which we consider to be less than comely and sometimes of some concern to the body. It is commonly called the "armpit". What do we do when our armpit becomes sweaty, and the odor is offensive? Do we cut it out and throw it away? No! We do our best to remedy the situation, by whatever means possible, because as offensive as it may be, the armpit has a specified function and is a part of the body. In the church, leaders must minister to those who are "sick and are offensive" to the testimony of the church. This requires using the Word of God to convict them of their sin, bringing them to a place of genuine repentance and restoring them in a spirit of gentleness; only then can the one who was "sick and offensive" be useful again in the ministry of the church.

Another very important point to note about the body is that it does not function only periodically. The various parts of our body are always working 24 hours a day, seven days a week. This must also be true of the members of the Body of Christ. They must also be at work all the time: early in the morning, late at night, in the marketplace, in the school room, the boardroom, in the downtown office, and not just in the church services on Sunday morning.

The Church is a family, through which nurturing, edification, discipline, and all of the other activities consistent with the human family, takes place. It is when this concept of "family" is missing, that sometimes we see a demonstration of selfishness in how we lookout for ourselves and scarcely consider the hurts and needs of those who are a part of the household of faith. We are however admonished by Paul the apostle in Philippians 2:4 "look not every man on his own things, but every man also on the things of others". This command, addresses our responsibility toward each other in the body of Christ. The effectiveness of the body ministry of the church is also dependent on the church functioning as an organism. Ephesians 4:16 illustrates:

"..From whom the whole body fitly joined together and compacted by that which every joint supplieth, according to the effectual working in the measure of every part,

maketh increase of the body unto the edifying of itself in love".

First we see that each member has a key role or function to play in the body that aids in the overall development of the collective whole. Second, there needs to be great diligence exercised in ensuring that each member is functional and connected to the whole. A member may be connected or located in the right place, but if that member is not functional, (s) he is of no value to the body. When the members are functioning within the context of their specific gifting and callings, the body will grow and develop the way God has ordained for it to grow and develop. It is important to note that while the admonition is for the individual members to be connected and function, the focus is not on individual growth, but rather, on the growth of the body.

Care must be taken to avoid the individualistic approach, where everyone promotes himself and seeks after his own fame and success, and not the overall health of the church. In this regard, it would be instructive for volunteer and staff members of a ministry to be made aware that, when given an opportunity to serve alongside your pastor, it is improper to seek to use that opportunity to promote your own vision and ministry under the pretense of supporting the vision of the pastor. The body will only do well, if your energies are concentrated on the single vision of the local ministry within which you serve.

The Church as Organization

It is argued by Tidwel that, " the church as an organism is a basic unit constituted to carry on the activities of its life by means of parts separate in function but mutually dependent" (Tidwel,1985). He further contends that, "a well administered organism is more usable by God than a disorderly one". It is against this backdrop that I begin consideration of the church as an organization.

When we speak of organization, we are referring to the church as a body of people, organized in a particular manner to get the work of the ministry done. The church has a specific mandate to accomplish here on the earth, and for this reason, there is an absolute need to have the work of God organized around some definite pattern or structure in order to be effective.

The Biblical premise on which the organization of the church is built is seen in Acts 14:23 and Titus 1:5. The appointment of elders to oversee the local congregation came at a time when the church was developing, and it became necessary to put systems and structures in place to continue doing the work of the ministry effectively. The elders (Greek presbuteros, from which we get our English word presbyter,) were generally the older men within the congregation. They were also at times referred to as bishops. The bishops or "episkopos" were overseers and their task was to oversee the congregation (Acts 20: 17, 28). Then there were pastors. The pastor or "poimen" was the shepherd who was tasked with the responsibility of feeding the flock of God. But the question is, does the church need to be organized? Let us re-examine the quote from Tidwell, "a well administered organism is more usable by God than a disorderly one".

When believers in Christ join together as a congregation to do the work that Jesus commissioned the church to do: How can ministry best be organized to allow the church to function and fulfill its purpose? The constitution or bylaws of a local church helps them stay focused on the purpose and mission of the church and help prevent them from falling into complacency and just "doing church." In architecture, one of the most important concepts is that "form follows function." I believe that in a similar way the form or structure of ministry in a church should follow the function and purpose of the church. We will now look at some of these concepts by starting with the head leadership of the church and working our way down.

Who is the head of the Church? The first and most important part of the church's structure is the Head Shepherd who is Jesus Christ (Ephesians 1:22-23, 4:15-16; 1 Corinthians 12:12-13). He is the one who joins and holds every part of the church's body together. Without Jesus as the head of the church, it will not be able to function or accomplish its mission. Underneath the Head Shepherd, there is a group of under shepherds (overseers, elders or pastors) who are the spiritual leaders of the church. This group of spiritual leaders can be composed of some individuals who have dedicated their livelihoods to ministry and others who do not and make a living elsewhere. Their primary focus is to oversee the spiritual aspects of the church.

We can see with the early church in Acts 6:1-4 that, in addition to spiritual matters, the twelve apostles also encountered other things that needed attention in the church.

Now in these days when the disciples were increasing in number, a complaint by the Hellenists arose against the Hebrews because their widows were being neglected in the daily distribution. And the twelve summoned the full number of the disciples and said, "It is not right that we should give up preaching the word of God to serve tables. Therefore, brothers, pick out from among you seven men of good repute, full of the Spirit and of wisdom, whom we will appoint to this duty. But we will devote ourselves to prayer and to the ministry of the word." (ESV)

This passage shows that the twelve apostles saw their need to stay focused on the spiritual matters of ministry. So they appointed deacons (which means "servant") to support and serve the spiritual leadership and the church by taking care of the other primarily physical aspects of ministry. Today these things can include church finances, support staff, maintenance of the church's property, custodial, technical ministries, and other "helps" or service ministries. This allows the spiritual leadership to not become preoccupied by these other things that need to be taken care of in the church. There is a natural tendency to get pulled into focusing on the physical world around us and end up neglecting the more important spiritual matters of the church. With the head spiritual leadership and supporting service leadership established, we can turn our attention to how we can structure specific areas of ministry under the head leadership.

If we want to form the structure of ministry around how it functions, we need to discover the basic functions of the church. Rick Warren, in his *Purpose Driven Church*, identifies some basic functions of the church, which we will now discuss. These functions or purposes as described by Warren, are drawn from two scriptural texts: Matthew 28:19-20 and Matthew 22:37-40. These two portions of scripture are more popularly referred to as the Great Commission (Mt. 28:19-20) and the Great Commandment (Mt. 22:37-40).

The five functions or purposes of the church as described by Warren are as follows: worship, ministry, evangelism, fellowship, and discipleship. It must not be assumed that Warren's contextualization of these purposes is the only biblical interpretation of these two verses. But for the purpose of this discussion, we will contain our interpretation to that which is provided by Warren. What is really represented is the relationship that the church must have with God, its members, and the community in which it functions. All of these relationships work together in balance and are necessary for each other to function properly. These areas outlined by Warren are all part of the various processes that the local church undertakes in pursuit of fulfilling the Great Commandment and Commission, and is overseen by the spiritual leadership. People come into the body of Christ through evangelism and then through equipping, encouragement, and growing in their relationship with Christ they then go out and evangelize others who are then brought into the discipleship process (Matthew 28:19-20; Romans 10:14-15).

With each of these relationships, ministry teams can be established under the church leadership to help ensure that each one functions properly and that no area is neglected or out of balance. Sub-teams can also be established under each of these core ministry teams to deal with more specific areas if necessary. Some ministries are organized along age or gender lines. For example, there is Women's ministry, or Men's ministry, or Youth and Children's ministry. The idea is to ensure that each person in the church can be covered by more than one group, and each group can minister a little differently in each of the four areas to a particular people group.

It is important with group ministries to make sure you do not create too many groups that are functioning independently. Try to keep groups that are similar together so that they will work better being with other teams that are related to it. For example, you could have a main Family ministry group with sub-teams for marriages, single parents, divorced, and grief support. In essence, all of these various groups and departments help to maintain order and structure while ensuring that the spiritual needs are being met, and the will of God for his church is being accomplished.

In some churches today, there is still the archaic view that the church is strictly an "organism" and therefore there is "no place for secular organizational structures. I believe that the argument is already made regarding the biblical premise, as well as the present value of good organization in the local church.

CHAPTER 4

The Church: Its Mission, Message, and Messenger

Its Mission

As was discussed earlier, the Church has been mandated by Christ to fulfill the Great Commission in the earth. First of all, I would like to discuss the mission of the church as outlined by scripture and to consider the views offered by some of our contemporary writers on this matter. What, therefore, is the mission of the Church? In answering this question, I must first point out what the mission of the church is not. The mission of the Church is not to become a political party, a pressure group, or a social club. While the church does have some social responsibilities, it must never be defined by the things it does in addressing those social needs. The danger, with which we are faced, is that in our attempts to attract people to our churches, we have engaged in all manner of innovative things, such as fairs, tea parties, pageants and fun-days, which have kept us so busy, that we scarcely have the time to be doing what we have been called to do as a church. It is against this backdrop that we must rediscover what the real mission of the church is. Dale A. Robbins posits that the mission of the church is "a continuation of Christ's earthly ministry". In essence, this points back to two very important scriptures, which are; 1) "Go therefore and make disciples of all the nations, baptizing them in the name of the Father and of the Son and of the Holy Spirit, teaching them to observe all things that I have commanded you; and lo, I am with you always, even to the end of the age" (Matt. 28:19-20). 2) "And He said to them, Go into all the world and preach the gospel to every creature" (Mark 16:15). These two verses are a combination of evangelism and discipleship which are the two main pillars of Jesus' work on earth. They clearly represent what the church ought to be focusing on as its mission. Jesus viewed that redeeming men's souls was His whole purpose for coming to the earth. "For the Son of Man has come to save that which was lost." (Matt. 18:11.) In turn, He imparted this same objective to His disciples. He said to them, "Follow Me, and I will make you fishers of men" (Matt. 4:19). A number of questions arise in considering these verses. Does the church of Jesus Christ really understand why it is that Christ came? Much of what we hear today would suggest that some Christians are of the view that Christ has come to "bless" them and make their lives happy and prosperous. There seems to be an obsession with "wealth and prosperity," to the point that Jesus is often presented in our sermons as the solution to poverty, debt, bank foreclosure, and everything bad, including a bad hair day. But we are here reminded in Matthew 18:11 that Jesus' purpose for coming is to "save that which was lost." I contend therefore that the church's mission must focus on seeking after the saving of those who are lost. ReinhardBonnke puts it very nicely when he said, "The fact remains forever that God's concern today, as at Calvary, is the salvation of souls." I rather suspect that one of the reasons much emphasis is not placed on evangelism in some churches, is because the real value of the human soul is not quite appreciated. One soul is of great value to the Kingdom of God, and this is demonstrated in the fact that Christ went all the way to Calvary to purchase our souls. It is also seen in the words of Jesus in Luke 15:7. " I say unto you that likewise joy shall be in heaven over one sinner that repenteth , more than over ninety and nine just persons, which need no repentance"(KJV). The human soul is of great value to God, and our mission as a church is to pursue the salvation of lost souls.

While the ultimate objective of all we do is the salvation of souls, there are a number of other things which the church is required of God to do as well. Jesus, while here on earth, preached the Kingdom of God and sought for the redemption of the soul, but he also ministered to those who were in need. Perhaps the statement which best summarizes this mission of Christ and His church, was given as Jesus read from Isaiah's prophecy in Nazareth's synagogue on the Sabbath day. He said, "The Spirit of the LORD is upon me, because He has anointed me to preach the gospel to the poor. He has sent me to heal the brokenhearted, to preach deliverance to the captives and recovery of sight to the blind, to set at liberty those who are oppressed, to preach the acceptable year of the LORD" (Luke

4:18-19). So there are a number of life transforming things that the church is called by God to do as we minister to a dying world. You may ask, "So what about our responsibility to the poor, and the pursuit of social justice?" Doesn't the church have a responsibility for these things as well? We do. But I must reiterate that our mission is not feeding the poor and pursuing social justice, it is saving souls. However, we will discuss a little later, the responsibility of the church in social and other matters.

We have considered so far, the first part of the commission, which is evangelism, getting men saved. But, there is a second part which is, "Teaching them to observe all things whatsoever I have commanded you." Jesus said, "Teaching them." Who are those that he is referring to? Teaching those who are baptized, teaching the saved, teaching them to observe all things the Savior commanded. Thus, Jesus named another mission of the church. When the church has made disciples, then it is the mission of the church to teach them what Jesus wants them to know. It is not enough to teach them the first principles and then leave them to their own devices - they must be taught to observe all things that Jesus commanded. Therefore, teaching the saved is necessary. I must point out that my observation has been that this aspect of our mission has also been neglected to some degree. In some cases, after being converted, individuals are not given the kind of follow up that ensures that they are properly built up in the knowledge of the word of God and trained as disciples of Christ. The result is that when adversity comes, many of our young converts are unable to stand, thus they return to the world from which they have been delivered.

Our task does not end at conversion. The convert must be cared for and nurtured in the ways of God. When sinners hear the call of the gospel and become Christians, they have faith, but there is something else to be added. Peter said, "And beside this, add to your faith virtue; and to virtue knowledge; and to knowledge temperance; and to temperance patience; and to patience godliness; and to godliness brotherly kindness; and to brotherly kindness charity" (II Peter 1:5-7). But we must also seek to enquire into the purpose for discipleship. Why is it necessary for us to be taught and instructed in the ways of God? Isn't salvation enough? It is also the mission of the church to provide a place for spiritual growth and maturity to take place. The objective is that we may more and more conform to the likeness and image of God. Salvation therefore is not the end of the road; it is the beginning of a wonderful journey.

It's Message

The message which the Christian church is mandated to proclaim to the world is one of hope, redemption and eternal security. The church's message is not determined or set by a social or political agenda, but rather it is rooted in the very mission and person of Jesus Christ. There are two basic schools of thought regarding the central message of the Christian church. The first school suggests that the central theme of the Bible is God's great redemptive plan of salvation. The good news of salvation and deliverance from sin through Jesus Christ is the fundamental message of the Scripture. The key components of this plan involve the following:

- God created a majestic universe and crowned it by forming the first man and woman in sinless perfection.(Gen. 1:27).
- Adam and Eve gave in to the temptation from Satan, and fell into sin and shame. The consequences of sin are obvious, but people everywhere still love to rebel against God.
- Yet God did not abandon humanity on its course to destruction. He chose one people to demonstrate his special care and from them to provide a Savior for the whole world.
- God sent his only son Jesus Christ to bear the awesome consequences of sin. God does not just blithely disregard sin, but he poured out all the terror of eternal condemnation on his Son in those terrible hours of suffering and death on the cross.
- In the resurrection of Jesus, God demonstrates his victory over sin and calls people everywhere to identify with this victory by faith in Jesus Christ.
- In living in this salvation, we know that life is not meaningless, but we live surrounded by God's love, and bound for eternity with him.

The second school of thought considers the main message of the Bible from a much different perspective. These readers agree that salvation is certainly very important, but it is only part of a much greater message. That bigger message goes far beyond the man-centered focus of salvation to embrace the purpose of all time and space. We may call this message the revelation of God's plan and purpose for the universe. Under this head there are also many basic truths:

- God in his dynamic and creative essence resolved to create the universe and delight in it.
- However, God is not the sole transcendent being. There is a rebellious and fallen being named Satan who opposes God and his plan. He deceives and undermines God's purpose everywhere.
- This conflict marks all history and results in two kingdoms. Satan foments disorder and all that is bizarre and sinister. Quarreling and dissension among God's people is often his most horrid device.
- In sending his son Jesus Christ, God established the decisive hour in this conflict. In his servant hood, Jesus was the opposite of all the pomp, pride, greed and egoism that Satan promotes.
- In Christ's death, Satan declared victory over God, but the resurrection turned that seeming victory into actual defeat.
- Satan still prowls the world, but he realizes he cannot win. God's people are now heralds of his present and coming kingdom. Gradually the contours of the final conflict emerge across the world.
- Eventually evil so captivates and enslaves humanity that the climactic end time of history arrives. Finally, Christ returns to

earth as the victor and God's kingdom is established for all eternity. The purpose of God's creation and universal plan is achieved.

In the context of the twenty first century, the message of the church is no different from what Jesus preached while here on earth. Jesus' central message was the kingdom of God. From that time Jesus began to preach and to say, "Repent, for the kingdom of heaven is at hand" (Matthew 4:17)

"And Jesus went about all Galilee, teaching in their synagogues, preaching the gospel of the kingdom, and healing all kinds of sicknesses and all kinds of diseases among the people. Then His fame went throughout all Syria; and they brought to Him all sick people who were afflicted with various diseases and torments, and those who were demon-possessed, epileptics, and paralytics; and He healed them." (Matthew 4:23, 24).

Many other references could be given from the gospels demonstrating that this was in fact the principal message of Jesus Christ. Many of Jesus' parables were about the Kingdom. He gave the secrets of the Kingdom to his apostles. This message, when understood, is the most relevant message for the needs of humanity. It is a highly attractive message, and will produce the greatest results of any message one could give. This message must once again become the central theme of preachers and teachers in these last days. When the message of the Kingdom of God is given correctly, the results will be dramatic, just as they were for our Lord and for the apostles of our Lord. For with the proclamation of the Kingdom comes the power of the Kingdom. Paul declared in 1 Corinthians 4:20, ". . . for the Kingdom of God is not in word but in power." For someone to present theological arguments with regards to the kingdom of heaven, and not produce evidence of the demonstration of the power of the Kingdom, is to miss the very essence of what the Kingdom is all about. The Kingdom of God is not in word but in power. Jesus was not the only one who preached the Kingdom, John also preached a message of the Kingdom of Heaven.

> ***"In those days John the Baptist came preaching in the wilderness of Judea, and saying, "Repent, for the kingdom of heaven is at hand." (Matthew 3:1,). Paul the Apostle also preached about the Kingdom. "And indeed, now I know that you all, among whom I have gone preaching the kingdom of God, will see my face no more." (Acts 20:25)***

It is important to note that Jesus also commanded that we preach the Kingdom of God. "Jesus said to him, 'Let the dead bury their own dead, but you go and preach the kingdom of God.'" (Luke 9:60) "And this gospel of the Kingdom will be preached in all the world as a witness to all the nations, and then the end will come." (Matthew 24:14) Not only do we have Jesus and Paul as examples in this matter of preaching the Kingdom, we have the assurance from Jesus' own lips that this message of the kingdom should be preached 'as a witness' or 'with demonstration' to the entire world. This is the main task the church has.

The question can be asked, what exactly is the Kingdom? There is a prevailing view that the Kingdom of God is an alternative term for "heaven." Jesus however taught that it could be in our midst on earth, and come to us now through His ministry. For example - the ministry of casting out demons by the Spirit of God. (Matthew 12:28) When Jesus spoke of entering the Kingdom he was not merely saying "going to heaven when you die." He was talking about entering into the Kingdom life here and now. This includes heaven later on, and whatever plans God may have for us on the new earth, but it is far more than that. The Kingdom of Heaven is not about "pie in the sky when you die".

The Kingdom of God is the place where Jesus is King. It is a spiritual, invisible kingdom which has made its presence felt to a degree in the affairs of this earth, but only to a limited extent. It is not confined to a particular geographical location, or to a particular religious organization. The Kingdom is truly present in a place to the extent that Christ is honored as Lord and his will done there.

We must keep in mind that there is an opposing kingdom at work. Jesus spoke of Satan's kingdom (Matthew 12:26). The Scripture declares that, "the whole world lies under the sway of the evil one." (1 John 5:19) Satan is called "the god of this age" (2 Corinthians 4:4), "the prince of the power of the air," and "the spirit who now works in the sons of disobedience."(Ephesians 2:2) Satan, operating through a vast hierarchical network of fallen angels, evil spirits or demons as they are otherwise known, exercises an astounding influence on the hearts and lives of men, women, boys and girls. The existence of Satan's kingdom accounts for the hatred, the wars, the stupidity and selfishness of mankind, the existence of false religions and philosophies, and the presence of every kind of perversion and deception on the face of the earth. Satanic influence is very effective because it operates in the background, and is generally not openly displayed. It is almost always covered under another name or philosophy.

The kingdom of God is in continuous conflict with the demonic kingdom of Satan. These are the two spiritual kingdoms which dominate the affairs of mankind and influence the lives of many. They are totally opposite in nature. There is no third kingdom. The kingdom of God only advances through the destruction of the works and influence of the devil. Paul said, "The kingdom of God is not eating and drinking, but righteousness, peace and joy in the Holy Spirit." (Romans 14:17). That is to say, God's kingdom in someone's heart will produce a state of righteousness before God, and the peace and joy of God will be known by that person. If people only understood and believed this, then they would make every effort to welcome the Kingdom of God into their lives, instead of looking in all the wrong places for the happiness and fulfillment they desire. This comment applies to Christians as well as unbelievers.

When Philip the evangelist preached Christ in Samaria, "There was great joy in the city" (Acts 8:8). Today the need is for such a tangible, undeniable, manifestation of the Kingdom of God in the nations of the earth. The message of the Kingdom of God applies not only at the individual level, but also at every corporate level. The key to it is the kind of faith that recognizes and esteems Jesus Christ and His presence above all else. Such faith esteems the Word of Christ above all other authorities, influences or suggestions. The result in every community is the practice of justice, mercy, love, faithfulness, favor and blessing. These are exactly the things that people in the world long for. Because the church has largely failed to demonstrate and to preach these things of the Kingdom people have been willing to look for them in other directions. Satan has thus been able to capture the hearts and minds of men with all kinds of false movements and philosophies. The implication therefore is clear. The church must preach the message of the Kingdom of God. It is the message of the Kingdom; the power of the Kingdom that presents real hope to this world .The reality is that the church has been subjected to a demonic invasion which has robbed it of most of the blessings of the Kingdom. These went on for centuries, but now, in these last days before the return of Christ, God is restoring the knowledge of the truth as contained in the Scriptures so that he might have a bride that is worthy of His name.

The Kingdom of God is not the same as the Church. There are churches where Satan has a large measure of effective control. The will of God is not done in these churches. This is evidenced not only by false doctrine, but also by a lack of love and the presence of all kinds of relational and personal sin. The Kingdom of God message tells us to bow the knee to Jesus and get the sin out of our lives (Titus 2:11, 12). The presence of sickness in so many Christians is again evidence that the message of the Kingdom of God concerning divine healing has not been preached and demonstrated as it ought to be. Sin has opened the door to demonic oppression, and unbelief has held the church in bondage. The lack of true anointing, which in essence is the tangible presence of God amongst his people , evidenced by supernatural works, in some churches is another proof that the church and the Kingdom are not the same.

It's Messenger

Paul the apostle, in his letter to the Church at Corinth, states that "within our community God has appointed, first apostles, second prophets, third teachers; then miracle- workers, then those who have gifts of healing, or ability to help others or power to guide them, or gift of ecstatic utterance of various kinds" (1 Corinthians 12: 28, 29, NEB). What is set before us is somewhat a governmental or oversight structure for how the body of Christ ought to be taken care of. Paul Walker, in discussing the role of the pastor in today's church, recognizes that; "Biblically the Christian ministry derives its essential nature from the person and work of Christ." In essence we see exemplified in the life and ministry of Jesus Christ, the characteristics of the various functions which are identified in 1 Corinthians 12. The messengers of the church of Jesus Christ therefore, do not get their identity from popular media icons or celebrities, but from the example of Jesus. It is important to note also that the messengers of the church are wrapped up in a diversity of gifts and calling, hence it would be improper to assume or conclude that one individual or ministry gift is the panacea to the spiritual needs of the church.

The apostles in the church are those sent to fulfill the mission mandate of the church. T.L. Lowery argues that the apostles were Christ's representatives and guardians of the faith. In the New Testament however, we find that the word apostle is used in a much broader sense. They were considered to be pioneers – missionaries. In today's context the church of Christ is still anointing and equipping men and women to fulfill this very necessary function to the body of Christ. The apostolic gift today, is what moves men and women to launch out into new frontiers and to establish churches in places where previously the gospel had not touched.

The prophet identified by Paul as the second ministry gift are those who are to tell forth and fore-tell the counsel of God. Lowery contends that the prophets are those whose assignment it is to hear God's word and speak it prophetically. They are also responsible for bringing to light any error and sin that may have crept into the church. Additionally, Lowery argue that the prophet are those who take the lead in opposing many of the societal ills which are increasing every day

The third gift identified by Paul is that of the evangelist. The evangelists according to Lowery are those specially gifted and empowered by the Holy Spirit to express the Gospel in such a way that people are led to the saving knowledge and personal relationship with God through Jesus Christ. We see an example of an evangelist in the book of acts in the life of Phillip. He was responsible for leading the expansion of Christianity into Samaria (Acts 8:5-8) and also the conversion of the Ethiopian official.

The last ministry gift that Paul identifies is that of the pastor-teacher. In some Christian writings these two gifts are separated. Lowery amongst others, is of the view that these two gifts actually go together and are really two parts of a single ministry. The Pastor is the shepherd –the one who leads feeds and nurtures the flock of Jesus Christ. From a theological perspective the role of the pastor is traced as far back as the rural and nomadic life of the shepherd which is illustrated in Psalms 23. However, the role and function of a pastor as messenger, is not confined only to the shepherding functions only. The challenge for pastors is to find a unified role in the midst of all of the things pastors do.

What really defines the pastoral responsibilities? Is he administrator, shepherd, teacher, preacher, or counselor? In this modern era, the pastor is subject to a great deal of expectations from members. He is expected to prepare and preach challenging sermons, and at the same time serve in so many other roles, such as referee, laborer, plumber, taxi driver, just to name a few. It is these kinds of demands and expectations which sometimes cause pastors to become frustrated and give up on their calling. It is important therefore to be able to identify clearly what the role and responsibilities of the pastor is, in order to ensure that we are not driven by unrealistic expectations.

Paul Walker postulates that first of all the pastor must be a matured Christian. It is clearly stated in 1 Timothy 3:6 that the pastor must not be a novice, "lest being lifted up with pride he falls into the condemnation of the devil." What I believe the safeguard to be, is not a matter of one's age. It would appear that what is needed is a level of spiritual dept and maturity which protects a leader from becoming egotistical and conceited. The pastor should also lead a disciplined life. 1Timothy 3:2 reminds us that "A Bishop then must be blameless…" It is important that the pastor be someone respected by society because of the disciplined balanced life he exemplifies. The Pastor must be a person of emotional stability. Titus 2:2, 7, 8 specifies that the aged men must be sober, grave, sincere, and temperate. It also recommends that the young men are to model a behavior which shows incorruptness, gravity, sincerity and sound speech. In essence, what we see is that the pastoral role requires some to possess a healthy personality which is not necessarily based on charisma, but a Godly self-awareness.

The most important element of the pastoral role as a messenger is that the pastor must possess a sense of divine calling. Professionalism while being useful in its own right has become an enemy of authentic Christian ministry. What is needed in the church always are men and women who recognize the supremacy of the calling of God above the perks and benefits which sometimes are the motivations behind some seeking such offices . The Pastor's attitude to ministry should be guided by Paul's declaration in 1 Corinthians 9:16, "For I take no special pride in the fact I preach the gospel. I feel compelled to do so: I should be utterly miserable if I failed to preach it". The pastor therefore functions willingly in the light of a sacred responsibility. It is this understanding of the sacredness of the call which qualifies the pastor, even in the midst of the complexities of providing leadership in the twenty-first century. It is not rare for pastors to become distracted by the many demands and expectations of the ministry and fail to pursue the primary responsibility of their calling. Pastors must therefore clarify what it is that they are called to do, and do those things. What therefore are those things which the pastor is called by God to do?

Acts 20:28 indicates " take heed therefore unto yourselves, and to all the flock, over the which the Holy Ghost hath made you overseer, to feed the church of God, which he hath purchased with his own blood. This of course does not suggest a literal interpretation that the Pastor's job is to provide for the daily dietary needs of his congregation. It however means that the pastor must be deliberate in ensuring that in his spiritual services to his people, he provides for them the information, material and guidance, either through counseling or sermons, to aid in growth and maturity. The pastor is to be a student, according to 2 Timothy 2:15, which says "study to shew thyself approved unto God, a workman that needeth not to be ashamed, rightly dividing the word of truth." It is foolish, I would think, for a pastor to assume that because he has attained the rank of a spiritual leader that he has come to the end of his education. As pastors we must continue to grow in order that we may maintain our ability to lead effectively. Growth requires that there be an exposure to new paradigms, hence the pastor must continue to study, in essence be a student both of the word and of life. Growth does not come only be studying, it comes also through reflection on the lessons of life.

Third, the pastor is to search the scripture, as is instructed by John 5: 39 "Search the scriptures; for in them ye think ye have eternal life; and they are they which testify of me." It must not be that the pastor reads a few verses here and there simply to add as flavoring for his sermons. He must be diligent and studious in searching the scripture both for effective sermon preparation and most importantly, for his own personal spiritual enrichment. According to 2 Timothy 4:2 the pastor must "preach the word, be instant in season, out of season; reprove, rebuke, exhort with all longsuffering and doctrine." The verbal declaration and proclamation of the word, is maybe the most important aspect of what the pastor is called to do.

Romans 10:14 warns that "How then shall they call on him in whom they have not believed? And how shall they believe in him of whom they have not heard? And how shall they hear without a preacher?" It is the bold, passionate proclamation of the word of God, flowing from an authentic life, filled with deep convictions, which will grip the hearts of the unbeliever, and strengthen the faith of the saints. The pastor therefore must not take this responsibility to preach lightly. He must preach with passion and with conviction, believing that his message is exactly what God wants His people to hear.

The pastor must also be a teacher. 1 Timothy 3:2 indicates that he must be, "apt to teach." The role of the pastor as teacher is to ensure that there is a systematic approach to discipleship. The word of God must be taught deliberately and systematically in order to produce Christians that are rooted and grounded in their faith. Care must also be taken to ensure that what is taught is also consistent with the doctrinal integrity of the word, and not merely man's subjective interpretation and opinions of the word.

Finally, the pastor is to be a pattern or a model based on Titus 2: 7, 8, which states "In all things showing thyself a pattern of good works; in doctrine showing incorruptness, gravity, sincerity, sound speech, that cannot be condemned; that he that is of the contrary part may be ashamed, having no evil thing to say of you." The effective modeling of the Christian virtues is something which each pastor must do in order to establish and maintain the authenticity of his leadership. The veracity of his message is only as good as the life he models before those to whom he preaches. As a model, he sets standards for himself and by his own example, calls his followers up to a manifestation of authenticity in their own lives. Peter Northouse, in discussing authentic leadership, makes the point that "authentic transformational leaders become strong role models for their followers. They have a highly developed set of moral values and a self-determined sense of identity" More than ever before, the need is for consistency between the message and the life of the messengers of the gospel of Christ.

CHAPTER 5

Profile of a successful Leader

What exactly does a successful leader look like? In fact, is there a particular profile which a leader fits into, that can be considered as an ideal leader? There are varying views and theories presented on what the elements or factors are which constitutes a good leader. The list is quite exhaustive, and depending on the particular perspective taken, the strengths and weakness can also be identified. The question however, which needs to be answered is, How important is it to have an understanding of these elements or factors, in being able to clearly determine what a good leader is made of?

Factors of good leadership

It is purported by Northouse that there is no one perspective from which to view leadership. In fact any understanding of leadership requires first an assessment of the various approaches which have been presented and discussed, and which form the basis of almost every theoretical examination of leadership. It is therefore argued by Northouse that there are four fundamental approaches to leadership, which are: The trait approach; the skills approach; the style approach; and the situational approach. Each of these approaches, provides the framework within which one can understand the: who, what, how, and why of leadership. In essence, the "trait" approach focuses primarily on the person involved in leadership. It suggests that the right person for the job is that individual who possesses the right traits or personality. This is the "who" of leadership.

The "skills" approach stresses the importance of the competencies of the individual. For example, Northhouse argues that, "problem solving, and social judgment skills" are central to this approach to leadership. I regard this as the "what" of leadership. It considers not who the person is, but what the person brings to the process.

The "style" approach focuses more on the behavior of the leader, in terms of considering how the leader acts. This I would consider to be the how of leadership. The "situational" approach gives focus to the situation within which the leader is functioning. In essence it argues that in order to lead effectively, the leader must be able to know, and relate appropriately with the various situations within which he or she functions. The situation will then determine why the leader acts a certain way, relates a certain way, and make certain decisions. I naturally will refer to this as the why of leadership. Let us therefore consider this against the backdrop of the question asked earlier: Why is it important to understand these factors, in order to recognize good leaders?

What is very clear thus far, is that a "good leader "cannot be defined only by his/her trait, skills, style or the situation. Hence it is absolutely vital to understand what the factors are that may therefore offer a frame of reference for "good leadership". One therefore will not make the mistake of judging leadership based only on the traits or style, of the individual, but as indicated earlier, all of the other elements, will of necessity be eligible for consideration as factors of good leadership. In essence, both the personality and the process, both the leader and the follower have to be factored in, in a determination on good leadership. In this regard, a very pertinent question comes to mind, which was also articulated by Rosenthal &Pittinsky (2006). Is it possible to have leaders who have similar drives, methods, and even have similarities in temperament, but because of situational factors, they manifest vast differences in their outcomes of leadership? I would argue that such a scenario is possible.

Let us examine as a case in point, the late Indira Gandhi. It is argued by Steinberg (2005) that Indira Gandhi was generally known as a quite, shy, and even aloof young woman. However, in the execution of her job as Prime Minister of India, she demonstrated a level of aggression and passion, and at times even being contentious and domineering, which many found belied her true personality. Is it that her true personality was being passionate and aggressive, or quiet, and shy? Or was it that her responsibilities brought out a side of her which was only necessary in her given situation?

What is illustrated here is the fact that in leadership, one may very well see the trait, skills, style and situation, all exercising some influence over what the leader demonstrates in his leadership. As such, a good leader can only be defined, having given regards to the four possible approaches which have been considered. So what constitutes good leadership?

In our time we have seen the emergence of great men and women who have impacted the lives of millions and have changed their world in ways that are unimaginable. The question which we sometimes grapple with is to understand if there are some special distinguishable qualities or abilities which these individuals possess which set them apart from others? Do one's faith and religion, or beliefs and conviction have anything to do with their success as a leader? I wish to provide a comparative analysis of two contemporary leaders and their style and approach to leadership, in order to determine what are the styles, behavior and or temperament which determine the success or failure of a leader. In this regard, it may be possible to determine what the profile of a successful leader may look like. The two contemporary leaders we will consider are Nelson Mandela and Jack Welch. We will examine the traits of Nelson Mandela as a political leader and Jack Welch as a business leader. It must also be noted that this analysis will not seek to examine spiritual traits or virtues, since these leaders are not recognized to be religious leaders. The focus therefore will be on their leadership skills and approaches in a non-religious environment. It is my hope that much can be gleaned from the study of the approaches of these two leaders.

Much can be said of Mandela as an iconic leader and freedom fighter, but for the purpose of this research , the discussion will focus primarily on his leadership traits and qualities which he exemplified both during the time of his incarceration and while he served as President of South Africa. In discussing lessons learned from Mandela, Joseph posits that Mandela demonstrated that distinction can be made between leadership by coercion and leadership by attraction. Joseph continues to argue that Mandela demonstrated outstanding skills as a reconciler in times of severe conflict. As a moral leader, his beliefs and convictions regarding others caused him to appeal to and seek out the best in people's nature. He was described by Lieberfeld (2003) as being a partisan and peacemaker with tremendous negotiating skills; self confident (Benson, 1990, cited in Lieberfeld , 2003); and persuasive (Koch, 1990). Oliver Tambo described Mandela as "passionate, emotional, and sensitive". Lieberfeld sums up his personality as being characterized by a high degree of "self-confidence, optimistic self-beliefs, and feelings of self-efficacy"

What we have examined thus far is an overview of Mandela's personality traits, which provides great insight into his leadership style and behavior. In analyzing Mandela's personality with the trait approach to leadership as articulated by Northouse, it is recognized that a number of Mandela's personality traits are consistent with the major leadership traits, enumerated by Northouse. Some of those traits are: intelligence, self-confidence, determination, integrity, and sociability. A great deal can be understood of Mandela as a person by giving careful examination to these traits. However, leadership cannot be understood only within the isolated context of personality traits. In fact, Northouse makes the point that an inaccurate assessment of leadership is to consider a set of personality traits without factoring in the situational influences. Mandela's development as a leader was heavily influenced by a number of factors which included his educational background as well as the years he spent in prison. What is useful to note is that Mandela's effectiveness as a leader was not only contingent on the traits he possesses, but also the skills which he developed over time. It is argued by Lieberfeld that some of the very personality traits which Mandela exemplified such as self-confidence, patience, and persistence also made him an expert persuasive debater. He, while demonstrating toughness, also knew how to use emotions tactically as an integrative mediator.

It becomes necessary at this point to be able to connect these traits and qualities of Nelson Mandela, with the process of leadership. While all of the above mentioned qualities are quite outstanding, they are of no great value if Mr. Mandela was leading no one, nor influencing some change in his community or environment.

Leadership must be understood therefore in the context of organizations; followers, and leaders sharing a kind of relationship in which formal arrangements and agreements are not the determinants of what the leaders do for the followers and vice-versa. In some leader/follower relationships, followers by virtue of their affinity to the leader will go beyond the call of duty, and commit to a higher degree of personal sacrifice to accomplish that which is in the interest of the leader. The leader in this relationship invests greater confidence in such individuals whom Northouse refers to as the "in-group" within the organization. The essence of this theory, suggests that if the quality of leader-member exchange is high, it contributes to better relationships, performance, and productivity within the organization. While Mandela's leadership is not in the context of organizational leadership, there is clear evidence of a very high quality of leader-member exchange. It is posited by Stengel that Mandela had a tremendous amount of trust for people, and in his personal and political relationships Mandela is able to establish and maintain rapport. In commenting on his influence and relationship with the people, Choi pointed out that in spite of numerous criticisms from other ANC delegates, Mandela gained tremendous support from his followers and it was evident that he and his followers were prepared to sacrifice themselves against the apartheid system of government in South Africa. This shows therefore that Mandela's leadership approach is one which if examined within an organizational context, would produce a very high level of leader –member exchange, evidenced by loyalty and a deep sense of commitment to the organizational goals.

Transformational Leadership

Northouse argues that a transformational leader is one who is able to "engage" others and create a level of connectivity which raises their motivation and morale. However he also argues that the leader himself is also changed by virtue of this enlightened morality. When considering Nelson Mandela, one immediately recognizes that the very essence of what he accomplished in South Africa, exemplifies transformative leadership at its best. It is contended by Stengel that Mandela, "liberated a country from a system of violent prejudice and helped unite white and black, oppressor and oppressed, in a way that had never been done before." What must be noted however is the fact that, the primary focus of transformational leadership is to improve the performance of followers and develop them to their maximum potential. Is this what Nelson Mandela was about? Was he concerned about development of others to their true potential? Ottoway argues that maybe the most outstanding thing about Mandela was his ability to, "focus on other's potential rather than their deficit." It must be that Nelson Mandela was concerned about the potential of South Africa as a nation, which was the driving force behind his advocacy and life's mission.

Morality and leadership

It is postulated by Northouse that Nelson Mandela possesses a very strong set of values and is a "deeply moral man." He is also known to be a man of deep conviction and is very genuine. The conclusion which one can safely come to therefore is that Mandela was influenced in his leadership approach and behavior, by the values and beliefs which consequentially influenced those whom he provided leadership for.

Nelson Mandela, from a trait perspective, does posses the personality traits which distinguish him as a transformational leader. Within the context of organizational or business leadership, he exemplifies the traits, skills, and authenticity required for an effective leader. His leader-follower dynamics is also consistent with what is required for strong effective organizational leadership.

Jack Welch is a name that is known and associated with successful organizational leadership. Welch served as the CEO of General Electric from 1981 to 2001. During his tenure he literally transformed GE as an organization, but more important to the field of business leadership, he created a legacy of leadership principles which have helped to transform many organizations today. Thompson (2004) examines the life and leadership style and behavior of Jack Welch, and it is from this research that we will seek to conduct our analysis.

Very early in his dissertation, Thompson recognizes that Welch learnt, "good values such as toughness, aggressiveness, realism, perseverance and a very strong work ethic." These he attributed to the influence of Welch's mother who sought from an early age to guide Welch into a life of moral and religious values and conviction. Thompson continues to posit that determination and self-confidence are key values which Welch possessed. It is also recognized by Lowe that Welch in his early years of involvement in basketball and baseball, mastered the art of managing competition and motivating performance. Welch also, in speaking of his leadership abilities, said, "From my days in the pit I learned that the game is all about fielding the best athletes. Whoever fielded the best team there won…it was no different in business. Winning teams come from differentiation, rewarding the best and removing the weakest, always fighting to raise the bar." Further analysis of Welch's leadership traits however would reveal that there was another side to this iconic leader which, while it brought much success to his organization; contradicted many of the values which he claimed to espouse. It is postulated by Thompson that a careful examination of Welch's leadership approach reveals that in spite of his verbal proclamations he had failed to "develop a broader moral horizon or contrapuntal values such as mercy and compassion." This is borne out in the fact that Welch in his early years at General Electric embraced a philosophy of firing the bottom ten percent of staff who was not performing at the expectation of the company. This approach no doubt brought much hardship to employees who had years of dedicated service to General Electric. It was observed further by Thompson that Welch demonstrated a constant tendency not to be able to empathize with others and their needs. Notwithstanding all of the above, the results or impact of Welch's leadership style and approach are recorded in the success stories of corporate business literature.

When Jack Welch took over as CEO of General Electric in 1981, the stock's value grew a whopping 3,098% an annual average growth rate of 18.9%. This gives an indication of the magnitude of the accomplishment Welch's leadership brought to General Electric. It would appear therefore from the observations made of Welch's leadership, that there are times when the situation within which a leader finds himself, has a greater influence on the approach to leadership rather than the personality, traits or skills of the leader.

Transactional Leadership

From the evidence presented, it would be most effective to analyze Welch's leadership approach and behavior using the style and situational approach. Inasmuch as we do see some amount of traits in the various sources so far examined, the style approach which emphasizes the behavior of the leader, offers greater insight into Welch's leadership approach. Welch demonstrates a task oriented approach to leadership which focuses on goal accomplishment and which seem to ignore relationship building. While the literature provided by Thompson does recognize that Welch very earlier on demonstrated leadership traits which are recognizable as charismatic, he however demonstrates in his leadership style elements of a transactional leader. It is noted by Northouse that the transactional leadership style is one in which the leader does not individualize the needs of subordinates or focus on their personal development. Vital to this leadership approach is the contingent reward element of compliance and performance by followers being contingent on specific rewards offered by the leader. This is what we see manifesting in the approach of Jack Welch, in rewarding the top performers and firing the poor performers in the company. In essence Jack Welch saw the bottom line, and the bottom line was General Electric. The people were simply the means to an end, and therefore his approach was to focus on the task. If focus was directed to the people, it was simply to motivate them in the accomplishment of the tasks.

Jack Welch, while demonstrating exceptional leadership practices in terms of his judgment and management skills, however failed to demonstrate leadership principles with regards to authenticity. It is contented by Walumbwa et al. that in the context of all that is happening in the corporate world today, with respect to scandals and improprieties, there is a greater need for leaders in the business environment to demonstrate authentic leadership which includes affirmative moral perspective evidenced by high ethical standards which inform decision making and general leadership conduct. Welch, I am afraid may by some standards, fail in this regard, since the evidence of Thompson indicates that he "ruthlessly pursued the ultimate end of success and profitability." This according to Thompson came with a high price of a "massive removal of employees, in less profitable parts of the organization, and rewarding those who improved the bottom line." The question which begs to be answered however is, does authentic leadership suggest minimizing the importance of organizational profitability and success? If one were to subjectively consider Thompson's arguments, this would seem the case. I rather suspect that the argument for authenticity made by Walumbwa et al. is not with respect to what the leader achieves for the organization, but how he achieves it.

A comparison of the leadership styles and behavior of Nelson Mandela and Jack Welch must be done with the understanding that these two leaders operated within two different situational contexts. Nelson Mandela was a political leader, with a transformative style of leadership in a country. Jack Welch was a business leader with a transactional style of leadership in a business organization.

Both of these leaders possessed self-confidence and determination. These are leadership qualities which are esteemed as traits that charismatic leaders exemplify.

They both had dissatisfactions with the status quo (the existing bureaucracy) and were passionate about changing the environment in which they operated. They both knew how to get people to do what they wanted, in as much as their approaches differed. Nelson Mandela used the transformative approach which is to connect with people in a way which "raises their level of motivation and morality, and helps them to reach their fullest potential". In the true sense of the transformative leader, Mandela was able to model the way; inspire a shared vision; challenge the process; enable others to act; and encourage the heart. These are steps which are outlined by Northouse, as being consistent with the transformational style of leadership. Welch on the other hand used a transactional approach which according to Northouse, sought to motivate by offering rewards contingent on performance.

Mandela was relational in his approach, placing great emphasis on building and developing relationships. It is recorded by Stengel that Mandela after his release from prison and upon becoming the President of South Africa, reached out to persons who were his adversaries by calling them on their birthdays, attending funerals of their relatives, and even including some as members of his cabinet. This demonstrates his relational approach to leadership. Jack Welch on the other hand, was task oriented. Thompson highlights a noticeable absence of relationship and relational values in Welch who after three marriages and children born out of the first of three, makes little mention of his wives or children in his autobiography, but speaks extensively of the GE mission statement, which "he keeps in his pocket", and uses such words as "aggressive targets" and "excellence" . This is indicative of the fact that he is more passionate about the tasks being done and the business objectives being met, than about building relationships.

The question which must be answered is, what impact did the situational context have on these leaders? In the case of Mandela, the influence of the environment did not appear to exert much influence on his leadership approach. It is evident that Mandela was deliberate in remaining true to his character and values. Even when the reactions and responses of his followers were not consistent; Mandela continued to demonstrate the authenticity which is consistent with his leadership. Welch on the other hand seems to have been greatly influenced by his situational context. It can be concluded therefore that Welch's leadership style was contingent on his situation more than on his personality trait.

Some very important observations were made regarding these two leaders and others who have also distinguished themselves as transformational leaders in our time.

Not all great leaders have had the opportunity to benefit from formal education or training, but some have succeeded nonetheless, by virtue of other skills and qualities which they possess. One such example is that of the former President of Brazil, Lula Da Silva. President Da Silva has been responsible for the tremendous economic development which Brazil has experienced in recent years. It was reported in the Guyana Stabroek News of August 2011 that "Lula enjoys a near-mythical reputation among many. Brazilians have credit the former labor leader with lifting millions from poverty during his two-term presidency. He left office with approval ratings of about 80 percent. Part of Lula's popularity came from surging growth and lifting millions of people out of poverty. Brazil's economy surged 7.5 percent last year, its fastest growth in 24 years. The point is that formal education is not necessarily a sine qua non of success.

Nelson Mandela and Jack Welch were both fortunate to have had the benefit of formal education. While the lack of such should not disqualify one from positions of leadership, it is evident that these two leaders benefited from their educational opportunities which greatly enhanced their leadership skills. While the argument made by Hogan & Kaiser (2005) that, " personality predicts leadership style, does have veracity , this evidently is not the case with Jack Welch. Welch, who seemed to be an amiable person by his close friends, demonstrated a dominant, almost ruthless leadership approach. It does not follow therefore that in every case, personality predicts leadership style. The example of Indira Gandhi is proof of this. Steinberg contends that Indira Gandhi while known to be a very sedate person was quite the opposite in her role as Prime Minister. This brings us back to the argument of the influence of the situational context on leadership styles and approaches. Some leaders are able to function within a certain situational context, but are totally incapacitated in other situations.

Leadership and management are not necessarily the same. Management is more focused on the administration of the process while leadership focuses on the person who facilitates the process. Indira Gandhi, while possessing a particular personality, demonstrated a leadership style which seems removed from her personality. This raises the question, as to whether there is a difference between personality and leadership style.

What is responsible for the success of organizations? It is argued that the following factors: talented personnel and management and motivated personnel, are key elements. But all of these factors must be held together by effective, authentic leadership. Authentic leadership is greatly influenced by moral and ethical values. The point must be made therefore that the profile of a successful leader must take into account the style, the situational context, as well as the followers in the process. Leadership cannot be considered in isolation; separate and apart from the aforementioned influences.

The bottom line of leadership is not production but people. Leaders don't lead assets and organizations, they lead people. While this may seem like a contradiction of terms, it does align with the views of Knights & O'Leary who argue that when leaders lose sight of their ethical responsibility to others and become individualistic in their approach to leadership then it makes the process of leadership problematic to say the least. Effective leadership therefore must focus not on self, but on others as exemplified by Mandela. Our analysis of Welch also provides a very useful approach to business leadership in recognizing that ineffectiveness must never be encouraged by leadership. I however do not agree with the approach of hasty firing unproductive staff, since it robs the individual of the benefit of personal growth and development through the learning process. Allio recognizes that "trial and error is a key element in the education of leaders". Welch's approach it would seem does not leave room for that redemptive component to be realized. Organizational leaders can learn from both models examined. The drive and determination for organizational success exemplified by Welch is valuable. But the follower-development, charismatic, transformational leadership of Mandela is also of great value to both business and non-profit organizations of this era.

A note of caution must also be sounded here. Transformational leadership can be seen as elitist and undemocratic. The potential for abuse is also a possibility. This is due to the fact that transformational leaders are generally driven by a vision and as such they can be driven to the place of stretching their followers beyond their limits of comfort. It is important therefore that transformational leaders be deliberate in communicating their values both in lip and life; in words and deeds. People are less likely to resent a leader's attempts at stretching them, if they understand the values which guide the leader's actions. Transparency, openness, and trust, are all important elements in authentic leadership. Effective leaders lead by example, by communicating their values and moral standards in their behavior.

The more a leader becomes self-aware and self-accepting, the more likely he or she is to be transparent in how his or her values are communicated. Part of what distinguishes successful leaders, is their ability to add value to others. John Maxwell purports that, "Perhaps the greatest source of respect for a leader comes from his or her dedication to adding value to others." A successful leader therefore is someone who is able to accomplish the organizational goals but also effectively adds value to those he or she is leading. The model of effective or successful leadership which we have examined in this chapter, while it reflects leadership within a secular context, also provides a frame of reference for leaders within the Christian community as well. The traits and approaches exemplified by both Mandela and Welch can be seen as useful to leaders who will impact their communities to bring about any form of transformation.

CHAPTER 6

To Be Salt and Light

The Bible uses several analogies to describe the role or the identity of the church, in its relationship with the world. One such analogy is salt and light.

> *"Ye are the salt of the earth: but if the salt has lost his savor, wherewith shall it be salted? It is thenceforth good for nothing, but to be cast out, and to be trodden under the foot of men. Ye are the light of the world. A city that is set on a hill cannot be hid." (Matthew 5: 13-14)*

The inference of this text is that the role which Christians are expected, or rather mandated by God, to fill in today's society is not one of isolation and exclusionism. In fact, there is no record in scripture which suggests that Christians are to isolate themselves physically from society. The church has unfortunately become so privatized and over-spiritualized that it has lost its "saltiness" even as the world around seems to be in a state of decay. Rodney Clapp contends that the church today has become so "church –centered that it has become sectarian and triumphalistic." The role therefore of the Christian community as salt and light is to preserve the world from darkness and decay. In essence, Christian leaders should resist every form of systemic evil which destroys or has the potential to destroy the quality of life in the world in which we live. It must be noted that the church does not exists in a sociopolitical vacuum; therefore the neglect of geopolitics in the life of the church is indeed tragic. Consider the thoughts of one Old Testament scholar on this matter.

"Over the long haul of the enlightenment, Western Christianity has been progressively privatized in terms of individuals, families, and domestic communities. By and large, out of bewilderment and embarrassment, the ecclesiastical communities have forgotten how to speak about national and international matters, except in times of war to mobilize God's people for the "war effort." The inevitable outcome of this privatization is to relinquish geopolitics to practical, technical analysis, as Joseph Stalin's question, "how many divisions have the Pope?" That is, if the theological dimensions drop out of international purview, and with it any credible, critical moral dimension, then the world becomes one in which might makes right. To some extent, that is what happened to us, because Yahwistic rhetoric in this arena of life strikes any modern person as mindless supernaturalism."

It is clear therefore that modern Christianity has adopted an approach which sets up fences rather than builds bridges. To be salt and light in this world is to seek for ways and opportunities to impact on the institutions which are a part of our daily lives. Let us examine again the concept of salt and light.

> *"You are the salt of the earth. But if the salt loses its saltiness, how can it be made salty again? It is no longer good for anything, except to be thrown out and trampled by men. "You are the light of the world. A city on a hill cannot be hidden. Neither do people light a lamp and put it under a bowl. Instead they put it on its stand, and it gives light to everyone in the house. In the same way, let your light shine before men, that they may see your good deeds and praise your Father in heaven." Mt 5:13-16*

"You are the salt of the earth." Salt has a number of uses and benefits in today's society. Could it be that the Lord is suggesting that in the same way, Christians are to function in their communities in the way that salt functions?

Salt is a seasoning agent, which when placed upon food improves the taste of anything, for that matter, that it comes into contact with. When we come into contact with society, our Christian values should improve the nature of that society. Salt provokes or introduces thirst and as Christians what we do in our communities must create a thirst in people's lives that can only be satisfied by Jesus, who said: "if anyone is thirsty, let him come to me and drink" (Jn. 7:37)

Salt is also a preservative, which extends the life and improves the quality of the life of food. Ultimately, with enough salt, those who do know Jesus, and acknowledge Him as Lord and Savior will have eternal life. It is noteworthy that salt which loses its saltiness is useless. There is no tolerance for those who have lost their saltiness, or their "edge." Without the effective testimony of lives lived out with integrity and consistency with the principles that Christians claim to follow, the testimony of our lips is useless. However, please note that this does not require us to be perfect. Knowing our sinfulness and knowing our need to confess it and be cleansed of it is a vital part of the Christian gospel. Then, as v16 says, "let your light shine before men, so that they may see your good deeds and praise your father in heaven." We are to be light for the world.

Light has its greatest impact and relevance only when there is darkness. It shines on dark things and exposes what is there. This is a call to the church to challenge evil within our society, however uncomfortable this may be. Having humility and servant-hood within our character does not mean that we are to be weak and uncaring. The light that we bring, is not our own light - it is not who we are in ourselves, but rather the light of God shining through our lives as the Holy Spirit works through them. This does not mean that the only subject which we discuss or speak about, must be punctuated with references of God and Jesus. What it does mean is that when the opportunity arises, we must share with others the light that God has given us. We must not hide our light. We hide our light when we stay silent in the face of discussions which are contrary to that which we believe. We hide our light when we accept and conform to behaviors that are not in line with Jesus' teaching. We hide our light when we do not demonstrate care for the needs of others, and walk by on the other side. These are often missed opportunities to let the light of Jesus' compassion shine out in acts of kindness. If we let the light of the Holy Spirit at work in us shine through, then we bring glory to God, and there can be no greater joy than being able to give glory to the Father as we go through our daily lives.

The concept of salt and light also addresses the issue of influence and impact. The task is to understand how we can impact or influence a world whose system we are called to hate. "Love not the world, neither the things that are in the world. If any man love the world, the love of the father is not in him" (1John 2:15). How do we influence a world whose values are fundamentally opposed and alien to the kingdom to which we belong? I want to suggest that the most effective way to influence the world's systems is by impacting the social institutions of which we are a part.

Governments

Christians can be salt and light by impacting on or influencing the activities and decisions of governments. The issue of government is mainly an issue of authority. In this fallen world the authority mainly exists to maintain order. Christians do have a right and responsibility to influence how that authority is managed and exercised within the nation in which they reside. While it is understandable that governments are organized and operate differently in various societies, the common principle remains that governments everywhere have the same primary responsibilities. Governments are elected by their people to first protect life, liberty, and the property of the citizens, or individuals within their jurisdiction, and to ensure that law breakers or evildoers are duly punished. According to 1Timothy 2: 1, 2, governments are put in place to promote social righteousness. While it may be unrealistic to expect all government officials to become Christianized, they are however, expected to conduct their public and private life in keeping with the basic standard of social righteousness. I wish to state rather emphatically at this point that social righteousness or morality is not possible outside of religious groundings. America's first president, George Washington greatly feared that America would become a godless secular state, and so in his farewell address on September 17, 1796, this is what he said; "Of all the dispositions and habits, which leads to political prosperity, religion and morality are indispensable supports. It is substantially true, that virtue or morality is a necessary spring of popular government." I insist therefore that governments must be guided by a sense of morality. Hence I find it difficult to accept that leaders, who have no regard for, or affinity to religion, can actually demonstrate social righteousness. The Christian leaders therefore must seek for ways and opportunities to influence positively the activities of government to promote social righteousness. The apostle Paul had a clear sense of the kind of influence Christian leaders are to demonstrate when he asked the question: "Do you not know that the Christians will one day judge and govern the world?" (1Cor. 6:2 Amplified Bible). Mark Beliles and Stephen Mc Dowell make a rather bold pronouncement that "The battle for God's earth is being lost today mainly because Christians have thought that God does not really care about such things. They fail to see that Christ taught us to focus our prayers, not on heaven, but upon his kingdom coming "on earth as it is in heaven"(Matthew 6:9,10)" To be the salt and light requires therefore that we seek for opportunities to impact or influence the governmental or political institutions of our nations. This incidentally has been the history of the Christian church. The Christian church was an active force in shaping the political culture of many nations in the past. In fact, it was the rapid spread of Christianity throughout Europe which overthrew paganism in the then known world. By 500 A.D. some 25% of the world had become Christians and over 40% had been evangelized. The Church therefore has historically influenced significant changes in history. Even in the Old Testament we see evidence that the priest and the Levites were the "clergy" and the judges of Israel were the civil rulers. What is missing therefore from today's church? Why are we not influencing our governments as we used to? I would concur with the view of Gordon Harland who postulates that:

" What is at stake is evangelical participation in the shaping of civil society-to recover the vocation of public deacons and encourage the new Josephs or Daniels to

serve in palaces and parliaments to secure peace and justice . Of course the very struggle to secure justice itself involves the use of the instruments of power, and the instruments of power are always ambiguous. Nor can innocence be maintained or purity achieved by withholding from the struggle. The fact to be recognized is this: there is no moral hiding place."

This view is also supported by John Eidsmoe who contends that "I believe the entry of evangelicals into the political arena is a positive step"

Church and State

The struggle which continues to create the confusion for many Christians and which in many ways has contributed to the attitude of Christians disengaging from participation or involvement in public affairs, is that of the separation of church and state. To have a clear understanding of how this affects us, we must consider the biblical background to this issue. Israel in the Old Testament was governed by a theocratic system where God ruled as sovereign. Under such a system there was no separation of church and state. God was in charge and his agenda was what human life was organized around. However, what did exist was a system of separation and limited government in which the Levites were the priesthood and the kings and judges coming from the tribe of Judah. Jesus in addressing this issue of separation of the two kingdoms stated in Luke 20:25 "Render unto Caesar the things which be Caesar's, and unto God the things which be God's." What seems to be the context of this remark is that the State is being given a certain degree of legitimacy as well as prescribing the boundaries of its authority. He in essence is saying, there are some things that Caesar has no jurisdiction over. Those things I suspect are the things which are sacred and exclusive to the kingdom of God.

The challenge for some is to understand how the church ought to relate with a kingdom controlled by Caesar. The preferred approach I have observed is to pick a fight and be confrontational and antagonistic. I submit that in order to be salt and light, there must be a re-assessment of our approach and attitude to government and matters of state. The need of this hour demands a re-assessment of the perspectives and ideological positions which have informed our attitude to such an important issue in the kingdom of God. Many have steered clear of any involvement or association with government or politics because there is the popular view that politics is "dangerous and dirty." If one were to consider the evidence of scripture on this matter one would see absolutely no support for such a posture. In fact one would see the total contrary.

Some of the most spiritual persons in the bible were kings and judges in Israel, which are governmental offices. Daniel was a prime minister in Babylon as well as in Persia, and there is record to show that he was a godly and upright man. Joseph also served as the prime minister in Egypt. It is useful to note that the ruler under whose authority these men of God served, were considered to be "ungodly." Darius and Nebuchadnezzar for example, under whose leadership Daniel served, were leaders who did not fear nor honor God. Yet these godly men served with distinction in political offices, representing the Kingdom of God well. The unrighteousness of the leaders did not cause these men to shrink from political involvement. Is this not the very essence of what it means to be salt and light? Where is light needed the most? Evidently, where the darkness is greatest! The influence of a righteous man or woman can only be greatly appreciated if there is the evidence of unrighteousness.

Even in the New Testament we see record of "Erastus the chamberlain "sending greetings to Christians who resided at Rome (Romans 16:23). The chamberlain is the same as a city treasurer today. The believer, who is elected to serve in public political office, has been entrusted with an awesome responsibility and opportunity to be the salt and light of the kingdom of God. Some would also argue that the role of the church is really to be saving souls and not to be out politicking. While there is great truth to this assertion, it ignores the fact that the church also has a responsibility for social justice, as is made clear by Proverbs 21:3 "To do justice and judgment is more acceptable to the lord than sacrifice." The efforts and activities of Christians must ultimately lead to the transformation of the human soul, but we must in the process work for the redemption of human society as well. What also needs to be said is that distinctions must be made regarding the role of the church as a religious organization, and the role of its individual members. While it must be recognized and understood that the church as a whole is not always the instrument for political or social action, there are some issues which requires a collective response by the church. However, I would advocate that in the interest of preserving the integrity and impartiality of the church, at no time should the church seek or even be perceived as seeking to take sides politically. The church can best serve as salt and light if it maintains its posture as an impartial, non-partisan plumb line in society. The church should seek to teach and instruct its people about their civil responsibilities, based on the biblical principles identified in scripture. What I advocate rather, is for individual members to use their faith, values and vocation to influence the systems and structures around them. Individual members should seek public office. Individual members should join political parties, and campaign. But at no time at all should the church be engaged as an organized body in political campaigning and grandstanding.

Clark E. Cochran in his work Religion in Public and Private Life remarks that "an effective public role for religion is often not in direct political involvement, but in public witness to what equality, solidarity, and mutual respect look like in specific institutional forms." The command to be salt and light, although given to all believers, will not necessarily see all believers becoming involved in public or political life. Those who do have that specific calling must most definitely avail themselves to answer that call.

Those who do not have such a call must be very careful in how they judge those with such a calling.

It is contended by Stephen Mc Dowell and Mark Beliles that Christians should not expect to have good government if righteous people who possess a biblical world view refuse to run for office, or are apathetic and uninvolved. In fact, they further argue that even if some Christians do not feel "called" to political office they should provide help and support to those who are so called to ensure they are successful in their pursuit of a kingdom cause. Their conclusion is that, "It is this neglect of Biblical duty that allows the ungodly to gain control of government and for corruption to come in free nations, bringing national judgment and sorrow upon our children." I conclude therefore that one very effective way to be salt and light in today's society is by influencing the political system which governs our nations. The evidence points to the fact that biblical leadership is the key to social transformation.

Family

Politics is not the only way by which Christians can be salt and light in their communities. The family is also a social institution through which the values of the kingdom of God can be advanced thus bringing about social transformation. The influence of the home and family on the development of an individual must never be underestimated. The home and family being the designated, God-ordained, basic building block of society have been mandated to secure the temporal as well as the eternal well-being of its members. God expects therefore that parents take full responsibility for the provision of the physical, mental, moral and spiritual needs of their children. Those who neglect this responsibility are considered to be, "worse than an infidel." (1Timothy 5:8) It is suggested by Paul Walker that "often juvenile delinquency is really parental delinquency." While this seems like a grave indictable statement against parents, it is often true in many cases. The Christian leader therefore must bring to society a model of family and home that contradicts the norm of what now exists. It is argued by Stephen Mc Dowell and Mark Beliles, "that which shapes men, shapes the nation." The kind of character and ideologies manifesting in the lives of men in government, schools, churches, in the media and in the business community are all evidences of the influence of the homes in which they have been raised. Another very profound recognition of the value of the home is seen in the statement by Napoleon who said, "What France wants is good mothers, and you may be sure then that France will have good sons."

Christian marriage is not in any way immune to the attacks and difficulties which marriages in general are susceptible to, but the indwelling presence of the Holy Spirit enables the Christian to have victories through all of those difficulties. The future of society depends greatly on the future of marriage and the family; hence there is need for the emerging of godly consistent examples of marriage and family, led by godly Christian men and women. Christians must demonstrate to this world that in spite of popular opinion, marriage and the family are still the building blocks of society. The transmission of Christian values to the next generation must at all cost remain at the top of the Christian agenda. To fail in this regard will have dire consequences not only for the church but for the nations of the earth as well. To be salt and light in marriage and family is to influence by our own example, how the institution of marriage is respected and honored. The biblical blueprint for a successful marriage can be found in the book of Ephesians 5: 22-33. Paul explains in this text how the husband and wife should relate with each other in their conjugal relationship. Often it is the neglect of these guiding principles which causes the collapse of many marriages. Believers demonstrate that they are salt and light when in their relationship there is mutual submission one to the other, in humility, gentleness, patience, and in love. The family that functions according to the biblical principles is a beacon and an example to society. Therefore the role of both fathers and mothers in a family must be viewed as having great significance to the promotion of social righteousness and national stability in any nation.

Work

Christians can demonstrate leadership as salt and light by their demonstration of good godly work ethics and a commitment to honest labor. Work can be defined as "honest, purposeful, and methodologically specified social activity whose primary goal is the creation of products or states of affairs that can satisfy the needs of working individuals or their co-creatures , or activity that is necessary in order for acting individuals to satisfy their needs apart from the need for activity itself." God expects people to work and be productive. It is made clear in 2 Thessalonians 3:10 that those who do not work should not eat. It means therefore that Christians should not be given to idle slothfulness, but are to be industrious and productive. John Calvin argues that "nothing is more contrary to the order of nature than to consume life in eating, drinking, and sleeping, while in the meantime we propose nothing to ourselves to do." We live in a generation that seems to think that the acquisition of wealth and happiness is an attainable pursuit without putting in the requisite amount of work. Dr. Myles Munroe, one of the most venerated authorities on leadership, articulates that amongst the seven things which can destroy a nation is "politics without principles, pleasure without conscience, and wealth without work."

As Christians our responsibility is to ensure that we exemplify honesty in all our pursuits. Human wisdom seeks to suggest that power, wealth and earthly fame are the only things that really matter in life. As believers we are to guard against such influences of pursuing material gains at the expense of our eternal security. Our motivation must not be to gain materially for the purpose of keeping up with the world. If that is the focus, it means that material things have become our God. Some have very foolishly and unfortunately sacrificed their values, morality and Godly principles in order to gain materially. It is necessary for us to be reminded that as salt and light we do not work to make a living but we work to make a difference. The Christian that is committed to being salt and light in their community uses every opportunity afforded to influence others within their work environment to a higher way of living and thinking. Christians in the work place are to lead by example in being honest, diligent, and Christ-like in character.

This also means that the quality of work which is delivered by a Christian must be reflective of the excellence of the Kingdom of God. To be salt and light means, we do not call in sick when we are not sick. We do not cheat on our income tax and we do not use company time to do our personal business. It all comes down to matters of personal integrity at work. That is what being salt and light is all about! An important question to ask also would be; "How do we relate with authority in the work place?" Are we respectful and submissive? The scripture teaches clearly how Christians must relate with authority in the workplace. "Servants, obey your earthly masters with respect and fear, and with sincerity of heart, just as you would obey Christ. Obey them not only to win their favor when their eye is on you, but like slaves of Christ, doing the will of God from your heart." (Eph. 6:5-6).

However, the believer must also be willing to stand up for what he or she believes in, even when the authorities within their work places are pressuring them to do otherwise. Civil disobedience is a biblical recourse for Christians in situations where civil authorities are seeking to enforce standards and practices contrary to their values and beliefs. We have an example of such civil disobedience in the Old Testament record. "Shadrach, Meshach and Abednego replied to the king, 'O Nebuchadnezzar, we do not need to defend ourselves before you in this matter. If we are thrown into the blazing furnace, the God we serve is able to save us from it, and he will rescue us from your hand, O king. But even if he does not, we want you to know, O king, that we will not serve your gods or worship the image of gold you have set up'" (Daniel 3:16-18). At all cost, the Christian must provide leadership in the area of just, honest and diligent stewardship in the workplace, as salt and light.

Witness

We have seen and learned through history that there are two dangers which the Christian church must avoid at all cost- separatism and worldliness. Many Christians believe that the scriptures actually give the license to have exclusivity in the way they live out their faith in society. Hence, there is a strange "silence" as it relates to the witness of the Christian church that is almost deadly. If the church will be salt and light, there must be a return to a deliberate public witness of faith and testimony of the people of God. We must recognize and embrace our Christian duty to witness for Christ in this world. In witnessing to the world the church must seek a common sphere within which the witness can be shared or take place, considering that we exist in an environment that is hostile to the message of Christ. It would be useful for us to first examine what exactly is meant by being a witness for Christ.

A witness, in the natural sense, refers to someone who stands in a trial to give testimony of an event, present facts or evidence and to basically support a case in some sort of dispute. If it is established that a witness is disreputable, their testimony is discounted or disqualified and therefore will have no bearing on the outcome of the case. A Christian witness therefore is one who by their life and testimony represents the truth of God's word and power in the face of a hostile world. The Christian witness must be credible or else his testimony will be discounted and be of no effect upon the lives of those he seeks to minister to. Being a witness is not just about standing on a street corner and handing out tracts to everyone that passes by. I propose the following as ways in which Christians can be effective witnesses as salt and light in their communities:

Seek to be like Christ- A Christ-like conduct is one of love and kindness. It is easier to win people into the kingdom of God by loving them than trying to preach them in. We are reminded by Proverbs 10:12 that "love covers all sins." It is sometimes difficult for people to respond to the preaching of the gospel if the messenger demonstrates an uncaring, condescending attitude in how he or she relates with the unbeliever. An old cliché states that, "people don't care how much you know, until they know how much you care."

Know and practice the gospel in our daily conduct- In order for one to be an effective witness he must become familiar with the life and teachings of Christ. In essence, he must know the word of God. The daily conduct of the believer must demonstrate a consistency that is unquestionable. Often it is that lack of consistency which casts doubts in the minds of the world regarding our testimony as witness of Christ. It is contended by Phillip Mohabir that, "over the years the witness of the church has suffered because of inconsistency. We do not live out practically what we claim to believe." This has produced a social dilemma in that the church which represented the custodians of honesty and integrity has become the object of criticism and ridicule as being a "bunch of hypocrites." In essence, our witness has become disreputable. The need therefore is for the Christian leaders of this generation to reclaim the lost ground by consistent Christian witness. Our conduct must substantiate our conviction, and our behavior must be consistent with our beliefs.

Become the solution- Mike Murdock argues that every believer was created to solve some specific problem on the earth. I suggest that this assertion does receive credence, if it is considered against the backdrop of Matthew 15:12, 13. Indeed salt is a solution to the problem of decay and light is the solution to the problem of darkness. The believer therefore must begin to see himself or herself not just as a candidate for heaven, but also as a useful, necessary solution to some problem which currently exists in the earth. The value of our influence is determined by the magnitude of the problems we are fixing. The greater the darkness, the more valuable is the light. If we can only appreciate this truth and embrace its implications, we would truly begin to see a transformation within our communities.

Often the Christian is the first to identify the failures and short comings within a society, and also to point out the deficiencies in the institutions around us. Crime and violence and the social disorders they create, are often the thematic outlines of many sermons. We preach about broken homes, and delinquent fathers. We preach about drug abuse and gang violence. We preach about teenage pregnancy and the problems with pornography. Where we have not been as diligent as we ought, is in seeking for ways of moving beyond preaching about the problems and seeking for ways to become the solution to the problem. The recommendation is that the church must begin to see itself as the solution to many of these social problems confronting us. We must be willing to move from amazement to engagement. It may require rolling up our sleeves, putting away our sermon notes for a while and getting down into the slums and ghettos, to extend a hand to those who are being destroyed by their own doings and devices. To be the salt and light, we must be willing to influence the functions of government either through direct involvement or through indirect supportive action. We must demonstrate a commitment to Biblical values for the family and marriage. Christians must demonstrate leadership as salt and light by their demonstration of good, godly, work ethics and a commitment to honest labor. We must recognize and embrace our Christian duty to witness for Christ in this world. And finally, as mentioned above, the believer must see himself or herself not just as a candidate for heaven but also as a useful, necessary solution to some problem which currently exists in the earth.

CHAPTER 7

The Cost of Leadership

Everything comes with a cost, especially leadership. The transformational leader will find that in order to make the kind of impact needed to bring about radical, lasting changes in a community, there are certain sacrifices which will have to be made. These sacrifices sometimes are of tremendous personal cost, and can have very grave implications for the personal, as well as family and relational, health of the leader.

Balance

The first thing the transformational leader must know is the importance of balance. The leader must be able to set and maintain priorities in his life. He must understand clearly that there is a difference between important and urgent. Some things may be important but not urgent, hence there can be a deferring of some responsibilities to other times, enabling the leader to focus on other pressing "urgent" matters. Paul Walker argues that "spiritual and emotional burnout comes from a lack of balance and management." Time management is therefore a key area of training for leaders who will undertake the task of bringing about transformation to communities.

If time is not managed, the leader may very well not be around long enough to see the transformation he has envisioned. Planning, organizing, and prioritizing, are key elements of the personal management program of a good leader.

Planning

The leader who will live long enough to realize his dreams of transformation is one who first sits down and plans his strategy to ensure he can accomplish what he is setting out to accomplish. Max De Pree insists that "the first responsibility of leadership is to define reality." Planning is simply defining reality. The leader must sit down and consider what is required to realize the results he is seeking and what resources are needed and available to get the job done. John Maxwell jokingly informs that; "A leader is the one who climbs the tallest three, surveys the entire situation, and yells, 'Wrong jungle!'" So many great initiatives have fallen apart because careful and deliberate planning did not precede the initial actions. The danger sometimes is that great visionaries can also be impulsive. They are often so fired up about what they want to accomplish that they rush into the 'wrong jungle,' and valuable time and resource is sometimes irreplaceably lost. Planning must precede action. The scripture also encourages us to plan ahead. Luke 14:28 states "For which of you, intending to build a tower, sitteth not down first, and counteth the cost, whether he has sufficient to finish it?" This admonition is applicable to everyone, not just leaders, but it speaks expressly to those who are called to be the decision makers in the kingdom of God. Transformational leadership that will change nations will require careful planning.

Organizing

Not so long ago, when I became a member of the parliament of Guyana, my work load became rather demanding and as a consequence, I was finding it difficult to keep up with the various demands on my time. I found myself missing crucial appointments and forgetting important deadlines, until it was forcefully brought to my attention by my wife that I needed to "get organized." Peter Drucker, in discussing time management, recommends that "one has to find the nonproductive, time-wasting activities and get rid of them if one possibly can."

The leader that will take on national transformation must recognize that in order to have the energy to pursue something of such great magnitude, he cannot be available for things that are of little consequence to his calling to national or community influence. Some of the questions which I needed to answer in attempting to organize my own life and priorities were: Am I not delegating enough? Am I making myself too available for non-essential things? Am I attending too many activities and meetings which are not aligned with my primary purpose? The challenge for me,

I must admit, was to have the courage to drop those activities that were sucking up my time but getting me no closer to my divine objectives. Because I consider myself to be a relational person, it was difficult to say no to some invitations and individuals. But the alternative to saying no is to end up failing to accomplish my God given assignment; which is not a risk I am willing to take.

Use Technology to your advantage

One of the benefits of the increase of knowledge is the availability of new technology. The leader of the twenty-first century has no excuse for not being able to effectively manage his activities and by extension his life. Apple and Microsoft and so many others, have made available the technology that puts into the hands of this generation's leaders the ability to manage his most valuable resource- time. The use of the internet for emails, instant messages and the more recent use of Facebook and Twitter, significantly reduces the need to run from place to place to conduct meetings or to communicate with people within our network. Most cell phones today are equipped with the technology to function as a personal digital assistant, performing the task sometimes of an administrative assistant to the busy leader. These new technologies can significantly assist the leader in the organizing and management of his time, empowering him to be more effective in the pursuit of his primary call of national transformation. It must however be noted that the use of these resources, if not guided by a disciplined and focused life, can lead to further time-wasting. There are individuals who have found that they have greater challenges with the management of their time, by virtue of the additional level of access people have to them via the cell phones, texting, emails, Facebook, etc. The caution must always be that the leader manages these things, or they will manage him.

Do it on your terms

One of the greatest challenges of leaders, who have difficulties with time management and organization, is executing according to priorities. There is always a tendency to respond to the baby that cries the loudest. A friend of mine once told me, "It is the lion that roars who gets fed." As leaders there will always be individuals around us who will attempt to control our agenda based on their priorities. Human beings are like that. They think first about themselves, and it's not a human flaw or defect, it is just the way human beings are. The leader must however ensure that he keeps in focus at all times what his objectives and priorities are. He must not procrastinate to avoid having to do the difficult things. He must act based on purpose and priority.

John Maxwell postulates that "Successful leaders live according to the Law of Priorities. They recognize that activity is not necessarily accomplishment." The transformational leader must recognize this law of priorities and apply its principles. He must act based on his priorities. The task of transforming a nation is an awesome one, and no doubt everyone in the leader's immediate circle will have an idea of how and when they think it should be done. The transformational leader must be able to listen and appreciate suggestions from those around him, but not lose sight of the priorities of his own vision. Like David, he cannot succeed using Saul's armor. The strategy must be one that he has settled in his own heart that will produce the results he desires. Delegation is a key factor in strong leadership, but vision while it can be shared, cannot be delegated. The visionary must lead on his terms, remaining true to what God has put in his heart and spirit.

Pitfalls to avoid

As was recognized earlier, when the leader fails to maintain that critical balance in his life and calling, there are a number of things that can go wrong. Leaders have lost their health, family, credibility, and some even their lives, because of not observing the rules and principles of priority and time management. There are certain biological and emotional gauges, which God has given to us. If we pay keen attention to them we can avoid some of the dangerous pitfalls of leadership.

Biological time keepers

The human body is such a beautiful and complex organism. God has placed within the human body certain "reactors" which very often send signals to the brain that something is not right in the body. Leaders are generally busy people and are more likely to neglect their physical health in the pursuit of their dreams. The requirements for a healthy lifestyle are as we know: to maintain a balanced diet, exercise regularly and to get sufficient rest. Many have been the cases of Christian leaders in particular, succumbing to various medical conditions which can be traced back to improper lifestyle habits. The transformational leader would do well to ensure that he maintains a disciplined life style regarding his health choices. To be effective in the work of the kingdom of God requires healthy bodies; and healthy bodies are only possible through healthy choices.

The pressures with which spiritual leaders are faced in this time, contributes greatly to the magnitude of stress related conditions that are affecting Christian leaders. Every effort must be made to keep our lives free from stress and sickness, if we are to be effective in the task of transforming our nations. The Christian leader must bear in mind that his body is the temple of God. 1 Corinthians 6:19-20 informs us. "Know ye not that your body is the temple of the Holy Ghost which is in you, which ye have of God, and ye are not your own? For ye are bought with a price: therefore glorify

God in your body, and in your spirit which are God's." The leader must recognize that rest and relaxation is a part of the rejuvenation process which is needed to function effectively in his assignment. Constantly going without opportunities to rest and have relaxation causes what is referred to in economics as "diminishing returns." More time and energy is invested but less and less of the anticipated results will be achieved. A vacation is a useful opportunity to rejuvenate and refocus.

Spiritual gauge

Busyness is one of the killers of a Christian leader's spiritual life. Leaders are so used to being out-front and constantly in the spotlight that sometimes they fall into the dungeon of spiritual dryness and moral bankruptcy while still very actively involved in leadership. This pitfall can be avoided if leaders are sensitive to the spiritual gauge that the Lord has given to us. Leaders are reminded, "Wherefore let him that thinketh he standeth take heed lest he fall." This is a timely reminder to all leaders that no one is invincible. Leaders are all susceptible to temptations and human failings, and require the help of the Holy Spirit to keep them standing in spite of those shortcomings.

The leader must resist personal spiritual power leakage, by maintaining a vibrant devotional life and intimacy with God. The tendency sometimes is to neglect those private areas because of the demand of public responsibilities. I must insist that it is a foolish compromise to make. One can only be effective for God in public if he is effective with God in private. The leader must stay close to God, and be very diligent in plugging up any area of spiritual leakage that can destroy one's power and anointing. We can fill our calendar with activities so as to give the enemy the opportunity to capitalize on our busyness and ensure that we spend very little time in fellowship with God, and it is under those circumstances that our spiritual receptiveness and keenness is diminished. The higher we go in our public life the closer we ought to remain to God. H. B. London Jr. argues that there are three steps to a clergy or spiritual leader failing: "Becoming isolated from accountability; living with unresolved issues in the home; and neglecting one's intimacy with God." Bill Hybels contends that

> ***"Our goal should be to monitor our spiritual, physical, and emotional resources so we can minister, by God's grace for a lifetime. God wants us to live so we can finish the race we've started. That's the challenge of every Christian Leader. Monitoring all three gauges - spiritual, physical and emotional plays an important part in our longevity in the role of pastor."***

Relational Gauge

The leader that will transform nations and cultures must have a clear and personal appreciation of his weaknesses and vulnerabilities. The historical path of Christian leadership is littered with sad stories of great leaders who have been destroyed as a result of not paying attention to their relational gauge. The first relationship I want to consider is that of the leader's relationship with his wife. The role of a leader unavoidably exposes him to all manner of temptations and distractions that can, if not dealt with, harm his relationship with his wife. It is not a rare thing for people of the opposite sex to be attracted to a leader. Sometimes people who function in positions of influence are the object of all manner of improper affections and desires from others of the opposite sex. In some cases these affections develop into improper, unwholesome relationships which ultimately destroy the marriages and testimony of these leaders. The need therefore is for leaders to be watchful with respect to their relationships with their spouses. Any neglect of the conjugal relationship exposes one to the pitfall of adultery and moral failure.

Sometimes it may not be that an adulterous relationship exists, but even the very practice of flirtatious communication is harmful to ones relationship with his or her spouse. The leader would do well therefore to set boundaries in his relationship with members of the opposite sex for his own protection and that of his marriage. One cannot be deceived into thinking that just because it is public knowledge that one is married, that knowledge alone will provides sufficient deterrent to improper attractions being developed. There is a degree of bold callousness which exists which sometimes causes people to think first about their own emotional or physical needs rather than the spiritual and moral implications of their actions. This warning cannot be over emphasized; the leader must guard his heart and his marriage from all external influences and interferences.

How can a leader know when he is stepping over the line? One of the first indicators that there might be trouble in a leader's relationship is when he finds more pleasure being out of the home than in it. Sometimes it is not easily discerned that that is where the problem exists. The leader may genuinely be driven with a desire to accomplish his work or assignment which he has outside of the home, and as such that passion may cause him to spend significant time away from the home. But if it is a case where work is done or there is nothing urgent and pressing to be done, and there is a desire to be out, this definitely is a warning sign that the relationship with his spouse is in trouble.

If the leader finds that he feels an unusual level of excitement in the company of another woman, other than his wife, that's another signal. The giving of frequent compliments and making phone calls to "say hi" or to "check-up" on a particular female, may be a sign of an improper connection developing. If the leader finds that he needs to leave the room or speak in low tones to receive a phone call from a particular female, it is a sign that the relationship is not as sound and healthy as it should be. These and so many others are signs which should work as a gauge to help the leader avoid the pitfalls of emotional and relational difficulties in his marriage relationship.

The Christian leader must work passionately to protect his marriage from moral failure. This is one of the enemy's most destructive strategies against God's leaders. It is absolutely imperative that leaders keep their relationships with their wives as a top priority. There is no honor in transforming a nation and in the process losing one's marriage through moral failure.

A healthy marriage is not a coincidence, it must be deliberately cultivated. My own experience has taught me that time, effort and sometimes resources must be invested into keeping a marriage healthy. Taking day-offs and spending time walking through the malls can save a marriage from decay and eventual collapse. Putting aside a book or sermon notes and lending a hand with the dishes or the children's home -work, may be the thing that averts an explosion, ignited by months of silent frustration. Many leaders are too busy to be aware that their wives are suffering silently under loads and waves of depression, exhaustion, and sometimes even rejection. The assumptions we sometimes make is that our wives do understand that it is the Lord's work we are doing and therefore ought to be supportive.

For some people, being supportive is interpreted to mean that the leader must be allowed to do as he pleases with respect to his time, with no account being provided. I insist that such an attitude may very well become an abuse of the liberty of one's calling and ministry. The Scripture does require of both the husband and the wife in a marriage relationship to submit one to another in the fear of God (Ephesians 5:21). The point cannot be overemphasized that the health of the leader's marriage relationship is of significant importance to his success in accomplishing his assignment in the earth. Keeping an eye on the relational gauge therefore is an imperative.

CHAPTER 8

A Transformed Leader: Transformed Nation

The demands of our time call for a level of leadership that is not only educated and equipped, but one that is also transformed. We have considered earlier in our discussion the profile of a successful leader and in so doing, identified some very important traits and behaviors which are consistent with good leadership. But are these qualities sufficient to bring about the kind of transformation needed in our world today? Can charisma and excellent oratorical skills affect the social fabric of society and bring a halt to crime and corruption, which are so rampant in many nations of the earth? I submit that there is no evidence which is available to substantiate this. Hence, consideration must be given to what kind of leadership style or quality is needed to impact and transform our world.

A transformed life

The leader, whose life will count for something, is that leader whose life has first been transformed by the power of God. There are so many examples of such leadership qualities in scripture, but for the purpose of our discourse, I want to consider Nehemiah. I chose Nehemiah because he is a reflection of the kind of leader most needed for today.

It must be noted that Nehemiah was not recognized or considered to be a prophet, priest, nor a Rabbi. He was not elected to any prominent position or office of authority by the citizens or the king. But Nehemiah had a love for and commitment to God and a deep love for his country and his people. Every nation can greatly benefit from men and women who possess that same love for God and country. The qualities which Nehemiah demonstrated distinguished him as a caring, servant leader. A transformed leader is one who thinks first of the plight of others before he considers his own comfort. Nehemiah was so affected by the deplorable condition under which his people were forced to live that he "wept, mourned, and fasted, and prayed" (Nehemiah 1:4). He was willing to leave the comfort and security of his place in the King's palace, to engage in hard labor for the rebuilding of both the walls of Jerusalem and the lives of the Jews. Only a transformed heart can be so deeply affected by the sufferings of others. The world needs men and women who would be so touched by the pain and plight of others, that they will weep, mourn, fast and pray, until transformation comes.

Nehemiah also demonstrated that he was a transformed man, through the spiritual transparency he exemplified. It is recorded that he took upon himself the guilt burden of the people and made confessions on his behalf, on the behalf of his father and on behalf of the entire nation of Israel. This is the essence of integrity in leadership. Nehemiah was not being facetious in his confession. He was very honest in his confessions and genuine in his repentance. The hallmark of a transformed leader is personal integrity. He must have had integrity for the King to trust him as his cupbearer. The cupbearer had the greatest degree of confidential access to the King. If for any reason the cupbearer wishes to harm the King, there are sufficient opportunities available. It must mean therefore that the King found Nehemiah to be trustworthy and a man of impeccable integrity to have retained him as his cupbearer, for that many years.

Secondly, the people were willing and inspired to commit to the work of rebuilding the wall, which is indicative of the respect and confidence they reposed in Nehemiah. I submit therefore that Nehemiah epitomizes the kind of leadership that is needed in these times. He was a transformed leader, who transformed his nation. What can we learn and deduce from Nehemiah's life and attitude that can be useful in our understanding of transformed leaders, transforming their nations?

Integrity is non-negotiable

Personal integrity in the life of a leader is non-negotiable. As leaders we must strive to be above and beyond reproach. Our leadership must be of such a standard that we cannot be condemned on the basis of confirmed evidence. Paul gives us a very accurate definition of what personal integrity is when he said; "I myself strive to have a good conscience without offense toward God and men" (Acts 24: 16). The Christian leader must not only be concerned about his relationship with God, he must also be mindful of how his actions are affecting those around him as well.

While we have heard it said that character is more important than reputation, be assured that a good reputation is also a necessity for someone who will lead others. In fact, the integrity of a leader is best developed and determined within the context of his family relationships first. It is argued by Schmidt &Prowant that, " the integrity of our spiritual lives should first be evident to those who live with us and know us best" All too often, Christian leaders demonstrate a public image to their followers, which is so far removed from what their families see in their private life. It cannot be emphasized enough that honesty and integrity are hallmarks of transformational leaders.

Serve your generation well

A transformed leader such as Nehemiah seeks not for substance but significance. They look for opportunities not to be served, but to serve. Many writers have sought to define and explain the concept of servant leadership. Without seeking to provide a deep theological exposition on this concept, permit me to offer my simple explanation of what I believe servant leadership is. Servant leadership is simply giving oneself away for the benefit of others. This does seem like a contradiction since it subjects the individual to the control of the ones being served, and therefore represents, at least from the world's perspective, an abdication of leadership. Jesus however addresses this anomaly by stating, "Whoever wants to become great among you must be your servant, and whoever wants to be first must be slave of all" (Mark 10: 43-44). One can safely imagine the reaction such a concept would provoke from our modern day philosophers of leadership styles-a leader who is the slave of all? This definitely does not fit the leadership profile of our modern leaders. But this is the leadership which Jesus insists will impact lives and transform nations. The transformed leader will therefore be one who seeks to honor God by seeking to serve his fellow men.

Earlier we considered the fact that Christians are the solution to some problem which exists somewhere in the world. The transformed leader must therefore seek to serve his generation by giving himself as an instrument of change, as a vessel to be used to rebuild the many structures of human society which have over time been broken down. Again , we are reminded by 1 Peter 4:10 that, "each one should use whatever gift he has received to serve others , faithfully administering God's grace in its various forms"(NIV). Myles Munroe contends that; "This is where servant leadership begins, when you discover yourself and decide to pursue becoming yourself for the benefit of your generation. Your service to humanity becomes almost a by-product" The transformed leader must serve his generation well.

You can't do it alone

The leader that will transform his nation must recognize that regardless of his gifts, talents and abilities, the task of advancing the kingdom of God, cannot be accomplished singularly. Nehemiah was burdened for Jerusalem, but it was upon the backs and shoulders of the men, women and children, that his vision found realization. Vision without implementation is dreaming. Transformational leaders are able to mobilize and motivate people to accomplish great things, beyond even what they thought possible. If we consider the great work accomplished by the indefatigable Dr. Martin Luther King Jnr. and the great Mother Teresa, we would realize that although they have been recognized for the transformational things they have accomplished, they both were significantly empowered to do so by faithful people who believed in them and the vision they carried. Greatness is achieved with the help of others. John Maxwell argues that "No one ever got to the top alone. No accomplishment of real value has ever been achieved by a human being working alone." This understanding is vital to a leader succeeding in transforming his community.

The people within our organizations and our communities may be differently gifted or able, but there is something they can do to contribute to the vision of transforming their communities. Therefore, as leaders we must not be afraid to connect with the people within our communities who are of like passion, who themselves are seeking after the transformation of the nations. As leaders we sometimes think that we are the only ones who carry the burden for the lost and for the depravity in our communities. I have found that there are many individuals, both within and without our churches, who are equally passionate about change coming to the communities in which they live. Many of them are simply waiting for a leader to emerge and start a revolution.

The need to connect and work with people however, is not only for the purpose of the physical or other support they provide to the process. Working with others in accomplishing a great and noble task, affords an opportunity for those with whom we work to be elevated to new heights of their own personal development. We add value to others when we make them a part of something that is meaningful and significant. A task as significant as rebuilding the walls, which is the defense and security of the city, is something that every citizen will feel a deep sense of personal pride to be a part of. I have found that people jump at opportunities to do things that are big or significant. The greater the task, the more the individual feels a sense of worth and appreciation for the opportunity. As leaders we must appeal to people's sense of Kingdom and patriotism as we seek to bring transformation to our communities.

Christians have an understanding of what the biblical standards are for the social institutions in which we operate; hence they are aware of the continuous breakdown which we have been experiencing. There is a growing discomfort amongst believers everywhere, of the state of many of our communities, and they are ready and willing to get involved in bringing about transformation.

Accountability – the protector

A very vital element of the transformed leader's life is the accountability network and structure which he sets up for his protection. Leadership, by its very nature brings a level of exposure and vulnerability which if not managed carefully, inevitable leads to the demise of the leader. Accountability is described by Charles Swindoll as; " answering the hard questions ....opening one's life to a few carefully selected , trusted loyal , confidants, who speak the truth –who have the right to examine, to question, to appraise and to give counsel." Simply put, accountability is taking responsibility and giving an answer for ones actions. Every leader must have some system of accountability established in his own life or he runs the risk of self-destruction.

We see a very profound example of accountability in the life of Joseph when he was tempted by Potiphar's wife to commit a sexual sin. It is recorded in Genesis 39:8-9, "With me in charge, my master does not concern himself with anything in the house; everything he owns he has entrusted to my care. No one is greater in this house than I am. My master has withheld nothing from me except you, because you are his wife. How then could I do such a wicked thing and sin against God?" Notice that Joseph recognized that he was answerable to both God and Potiphar for his actions. While it is expected that Christian leaders ought to be guided by their personal integrity, the presence of an accountability relationship helps greatly in keeping leaders particularly in times of personal challenges and temptations, to remain true to those inner values. Leadership has a way of causing individuals to move into areas of excesses, be it in terms of the abuse of power or giving in to the carnal nature. Many good leaders both in and out of the Christian community have become the victims of moral failure, as the benefits and privileges of leadership takes control of their unbridled affections. Having someone who is willing to provide checks and balances in our lives is vital. An accountability partner will enquire into our use of time, family relationships, relationships with the opposite sex, and our spending habits, just to name a few of the key areas of failure. But it must not be construed that the accountability relationship is simply for the purpose of "policing" the leader. It is argued by Schmidt and Prowant that the accountability relationship helps to prevent excess, strengthens the personal integrity of the leader, helps to develop discipline, and it provides encouragement for the leader when the going gets tough. The point which must be stressed however, is that those who are in leadership must constantly and consistently be reminded that their ultimate and prime responsibility is to be accountable to God.

In order for the accountability relationship to work well, it must be something that the leader submits to totally. In essence, there must not be areas of the leader's life that are considered private and off limits to the accountability partner. There must be honesty and openness about even issues which may be of a personal and embarrassing nature. I have seen cases of people not being totally open and honest in an accountability relationship, and the very things that the individual sought to withhold as a secret, was what the enemy used to bring about their demise. The enemy shrouds himself in anonymity. Anything that is a secret has the potential of harming us. When it is exposed to a caring accountability relationship, the enemy cannot use it against us. Transformed leaders will submit themselves to accountability relationships for their own protection and growth.

Its takes Vision and commitment

What was remarkable about Nehemiah's approach as a leader was the fact that what he saw when he got to Jerusalem did not alter his plans or his focus. In effect, Nehemiah had an enduring vision. He had a clear mental picture of what he intended to accomplish for his people. In order for transformation to take place in our communities, leaders must have a vision of what could be, and not be negatively influenced by what exists. There is enough negativity and cynicism around to cause even those who have committed to making a difference to draw back in frustration and resignation. But a leader with a vision, whose mind is made up about being an agent of change, can become the catalyst of a great national transformation.

The transformed leader must be synchronized with the agenda of heaven, in order to overcome the inevitable challenges facing this generation. He must settle in his mind that the task of transforming a nation for the glory of God will attract a level of satanic assault and warfare previously unimaginable. Remember Nehemiah 2:10. "When Sanballat the Horonite and Tobiah the servant the Ammonite, heard it, it grieved them exceedingly that there was come a man to seek the welfare of the children of Israel."(KJV) The enemy of our souls will not give rest to any man or woman who seeks for the liberation of the souls of men. Any man or woman, who seeks after the welfare of the nations of the earth, will cause the enemy to be exceedingly grieved. But like a soldier in the heat of the battle, the transformational leader must see beyond the immediate and press toward the ultimate. He must refuse to bow to the Sanballats and Tobiahs of his day and stay on the wall of divine endeavors. He must be courageous and consistent, committed to the heavenly vision of national transformation. God is faithful to reward consistency and commitment. To accomplish the task of transforming our communities, the transformed leader must have a vision and remain resolutely committed to its fulfillment.

What will a transformed nation look like?

When we speak of a transformed community or nation, we are speaking of a nation or community that has been so impacted by the power of God where Jesus Christ becomes the center of the life of its people. It is a place where the values of the kingdom are inculcated in people and institutions, which is manifested in behavioral changes in its people. Such transformation will also see a manifestation of economic sufficiency, social peace, public justice, national righteousness, and a continued acknowledgement of the lordship of Jesus Christ over the nation. A transformed nation is one where Christ is Lord over all spheres of society. In effect it will be the realization of Revelation 11:15 "The Kingdom of the world has become the kingdom of our Lord and of His Christ; and he shall reign forever and ever."

I should caution that a transformed nation is not necessarily a nation which resembles paradise. Poverty, hardship, and crime are realities that will remain with us for a long time yet. We may continue to see balance of payment deficits, corruption in governments and a number of other ills which are the current realities of most nations. As long as sin still exists in this world, we will be confronted with these issues. However, we must remember that peace is not necessarily the absence of war or conflict. It really is primarily a state of well-being and freedom from anxiety. It involves goodwill and harmony in human relationships. When a nation is transformed through the influence of Biblical leadership, there will emerge a level of civility and brotherhood amongst the people of that nation that only comes through the influence of the Prince of Peace.

In most countries where poverty is rampant, social unrest can also be found. Look at countries such as Sri Lanka, Vietnam, and Cambodia; just to list a few. These countries have been stunted by continuing civil war and conflicts. An examination of scripture will also reveal that the same pattern prevails. Progress only comes to nations that are at peace. So, a transformed nation must enjoy peace from war and conflict.

Jeremiah told the exiles in Babylon to "pray for the welfare of the city where I sent you...for in its peace you will have peace" (Jeremiah 29:7). It is evident therefore that political and economic advocacy is an integral part of the ministry of the body of Christ to ensure that just and favorable structures and systems are in place in the nations of the earth. The freedom of the church to pursue and accomplish the work of the Great Commission can be affected if the structures and systems of the state are hostile to the cause of the kingdom of God. The church cannot take for granted the opportunities which may be afforded to engage the political and economic systems of the nation, to bring into effect the rule of God.

The Biblical foundation for social peace is justice. This divine concern is so serious that in the Old Testament, the word and related terms are used about 500 times It is virtually impossible to expect to have social peace if there is no justice in the society. It may be that the level of social peace is consistent with the quality of justice. The Psalmist declared of God, "The Lord loves righteousness and justice; the earth is full of his unfailing love" (Psalms 33:5 NIV). Justice basically has three components. First in a just society, there must be equitable and fair legislation for all. In a transformed nation, the legislative framework must seek to ensure that there is common grace available to all regardless of race or religious considerations. If a legislative edict takes away ones right and freedom to worship, such a society is unjust, and needs to be transformed.

Second, justice must be concerned with penalty as well. In order for justice to exist, the penalty of law must be equally applied to the guilty whether the person is rich or poor, is of high or low rank in society, or independent on what friends the guilty may have in high places. Additionally the penalty must be commensurate with the offense. A transformed nation will not manifest such miscarriages of justice, where the rich and affluent in society are able to secure freedom, having been deemed guilty of a transgression, solely because of a bribe or gift given in exchange. Such corrupt dealings are the daily occurrences in many nations particularly those that are poor and underdeveloped.

Another very important aspect of national transformation is that of national healing and reconciliation. In some countries, there are protracted racial or ethnic conflicts which have built up permanent walls of division amongst the various people groups in that nation. Guyana, the nation of my birth, is one such nation. Guyana has a very rich cultural past, but one which is mired in a very painful history as well. Guyana's demographic composition is divided along six distinct ethnic groups. The two major groups are the Africans, and the East Indians. The East Indians constitute some 51% of the population and the Africans are 43%. Over the years, political elements have used this ethnic divide to create political control and as a consequence, began a cycle of racial conflict which continues to affect Guyana even to this day. The impact of this racial conflict has caused many violent confrontations between the races, particularly during and after the national elections, conducted every five years. What is important to note is that this racial conflict has sometimes even manifested in the religious life of the country, where there is evidence of racial undertones in some churches primarily in the rural communities.

A transformed Guyana therefore would be one in which there is healing and reconciliation amongst these two people groups. Because the church is a community of reconciliation it must manifest as its primary ministry that of reconciliation. 2 Corinthians 5: 18-19 reminds us, "And all things are of God, who hath reconciled us to himself by Jesus Christ, and hath given to us the ministry of reconciliation; to wit that God was in Christ , reconciling the world unto himself , not imputing their trespasses unto them ; and hath committed unto us the ministry of reconciliation." The nation of Guyana has been fractured for so long by racial and political conflict, that some have come to expect very little from this country in terms of national unity.

I submit that Guyana's future is not predicated on her past, hence change can and will come. Change will come when leaders who have been transformed by the power of God, begin to emerge and influence the social and political institutions and systems of this country. However, truth and justice must be factored into any process of reconciliation. If one group recognizes that a wrong was done, repentance should take place. Often this is not done. There is sometimes great reluctance particularly on the part of politicians to take responsibility for actions which have been harmful and divisive. This is where the influence of the church must be experienced. The Church, like Nehemiah, must take responsibility for the confession of the sins of national leaders, even if there is a failure on their part to do so. The wrath and the judgment of God sometimes are averted from a nation when the church begins to cry out in repentance. It is made clear in 2 Chronicles 7:14 that, "If my people which are called by my name shall humble themselves, and pray and seek my face , and turn from their wicked ways ;then will I hear from heaven, and will forgive their sin, and will heal their land." The long road to lasting social transformation begins in the church. The ministry of reconciliation must work first in the church and then, and only then, can the church be considered qualified as arbiters of peace and justice in our societies.

The Christian Church as the community of reconciled people to God by grace must become ambassadors of peace where there is conflict and unrest. Then can we be called followers of the Prince of Peace. Then can we be called according to Isaiah 58:12 "The repairer of the breach, the restorer of paths to dwell in."

Conclusion

The need of the hour in which we live continues to be for biblical leadership. While there is no shortage of resource and facilities to develop management skills in the work force, there seem to be an absence of the quality of leadership that creates transformative cultures within society. The evidence presented in this dissertation recognizes that the absence of such transformational leadership qualities have led to significant failures in many of the social institutions of human society. The family, government, education, the economy, and even religious institutions are all in search of solutions to many of the complex challenges which are facing them. The responses to some of these challenges have not yielded the results anticipated, but in fact in some cases, have even exacerbated the problems. The argument here put forward, recommends that the solution for many of these challenges can be found in the emerging of Christian men and women, whose lives have been transformed by the power of God, applying the principles of biblical leadership. The nations of the earth need to experience the courage and confidence of the Elijahs of this generation; the commitment of the Nehemiahs; the excellence and wisdom of the Josephs. Biblical leadership in action is the key to the transformation of our sin-worn societies. Men and women of integrity, committed to the cause of bettering the lives of humanity, are the needs of this time. It may be that such men and women do not necessarily occupy the offices of pastor or teacher or prophet within a local church. Or it may be that they do. The role of a transformational leader is not limited to those who function only within the context of church leadership. The transformational leader, who will impact on the social, institutional structures and system, is a man or woman, having a call of God upon his or her life to transform the nations of the earth. Such a person could be a pastor or politician. He or she could be a lawyer or a layman. The vocation of the individual is not the issue. What is of greatest importance is that the individual understands that whatever they do as a means of daily employment for a living, is not the definition of their calling and divine assignment. The cab driver and the congressman are both transformational leaders if they seek to use the opportunities given to them to influence and impact the systems and structures within which they exist.

The vocation is the vehicle we use to infiltrate the systems of this world, and to bring the influence of the kingdom of God to bear. Romans 8:19 challenges us to action. "For the earnest expectation of the creature waited for the manifestation of the sons of God." May the sons of God; transformational leaders, be the agents of change in a global transformation.

Bibliography

Allio, R.J. "Leadership Development : Teaching versus Learning". Available From: http://www.jstor.org.ezproxy.liv.ac.uk/stable/pdfplus/3792311.pdf?acceptTC=true. 2005

Bradshaw, Corey. "Global evidence that deforestation amplifies flood risks and severity in the developing world." Estimates of Catastrophic flood in Guyana. 1990 to 2010 .

Brueggemann, W. Theology of the Old Testament (Minneapolis: Fortress Press) 1997.

Bonnke, Reinhard. Evangelism by Fire.Kingsway Publication. 1990

Blanchard, Ken. "Great-Quotes.com."Gledhill Enterprises, 2011. December. 2011. http://www.great-quotes.com/quote/819728

Barret, David . Cosmos, Chaos , and Gospel , a Chronology of World Evangelization from Creation to New Generation . Birmingham, AL:New Hope ,1987.

Climate Science. "New Analysis Reproduces Graph of Late 20th Century Temperature Rise". (Online) Available From: http://www.realclimate.org/index.php/archives. May 11, 2005.

Calvin, John. Commentary on the First Book of Moses called Genesis (Baker House Company) 1979.

Clapp, R. A Peculiar People (Illinois: Intervarsity Press) 1996.

Cochran, Clarke E. Religion in Public and Private Life. New York: Routledge, 1990.

Choi, S. "Democratic Leadership: The Lessons of Exemplary Models for Democratic Governance". 2007

Covey, Stephen. R. Principle-Centered Leadership. Simon & Schuster. 1990.

Drucker, Peter F. The Practice of Management.HarperCollins Publishers Inc. 1954.

Drucker, Peter F. "Time Management" (Cited in Leadership Handbook of Management and Administration) BakerBooks. Michigan.2007

De Pree , Max. Leadership is an Art. Doubleday. 1989

Eims , Leroy. Be The Leader You Were Meant to Be.

Eidsmoe , John. God and Caesar: Christian Faith and Political action. Crossway Books. 1984

Greenspan, Alan. "We will never have a perfect model of Risk." Financial Times.(Online). http://www.ft.com/cms/s/0/edbdbcf6-f360-11dc-b6bc-0000779fd2ac.html#axzz1A4iS4eON. March 16 ,2008.

Hybels , Bill. "Responsibility to Self".(Leadership Handbook of Management and Administration.Bakerbooks. Michigan. 2007

Hookumchand , Gabrielle. "Conflicts between East Indians and Blacks in Trinidad and Guyana".Introduction to Caribbean History. 2000.

Harland, G .Christian faith and society (Alberta: The University of Calgary Press) 1988.

Joseph, J.A. "ETHICS AND DIPLOMACY: WHAT I LEARNED FROM NELSON MANDELA". Negotiation Journal. 2006

Kossoff, Leslie L. "From Manager to Leader".Accessed From: http://management.about.com/od/leadership/a/FromMgr2Ldr05.htm. 2008.

Kotter, John. A force for Change: How leadership Differs from Management. New York: Free Press. 1990.

Knights, D & O' Leary, M. "Leadership, Ethics and Responsibility to others". Journal of Business Ethics. 2006.

Lowery, T.L. Gifted to Serve. Whitaker House. 1997

Lowe, J. Jack Welch Speaks. New York. John Wiley and Sons. 1998.

Lieberfeld, D. "Nelson Mandela: Partisan and Peacemaker". Negotiation Journal. 2003.

Mc Dowell, Stephen &Beliles, Mark. Liberating the Nations. Providence Foundation. 1995.

Maxwell, John C.. Leadership Gold. Thomas Nelson. 2008.

Maxwell, John C. The 21 Irrefutable Laws of Leadership. Thomas Nelson. 1998.

Munroe, Myles. In Charge: Finding the Leader within You. Faith Words .2008.

Murdock , Mike. Seeds of Wisdom on Problem Solving.Wisdom International .2001.

Miroslav, Volf. Work In The Spirit (Oxford : Oxford University Press, 1991.

Marshal , Paul. Thine is the Kingdom .Vancouver: Regent College Bookstore.1984.

National Geographic Society."Effects of Global warming". Available Online From: http://environment.nationalgeographic.com/environm .1996-2010.

Northouse ,Peter G. Leadership Theory and Practice . Sage Publication . 2010.

Ottoway, D. Chained together: Mandela, de Klerk, and the struggle to remake South Africa. New York: Times Books. 1993

Orr, Robert A. The Essentials for Effective Christian Leadership Development. Leadership Essentials Press. Canada. 1993

Predpall, Daniel F. "Developing Quality Improvement Processes In Consulting Engineering Firms', Journal of Management in Engineering", pp 30-31, May-June 194.

Robbins, A.D. What People ask about the Church. Victorious Publications, Grass Valley, CA 95949. 1995.

Singh, Hera. "Confronting Colonialism and Racism : Fanon and Gandhi". HUMAN ARCHITECTURE: JOURNAL OF THE SOCIOLOGY OF SELF-KNOWLEDGE. 2007.

Schmidt, Wayne &Prowant, Yvonne. Accountability: Becoming People of Integrity. Wesley Press. 1991.

Serwer, A. "A rare skeptic takes on the cult of GE Fortune".
  http://www.jstor.org.ezproxy.liv.ac.uk/stable/pdfplus/
  3792311.pdf?acceptTC=true 2001

Stengel, R. "Mandela His 8 lessons of Leadership". 2008.

Slater, Rosalie J. "Teaching and Learning America's Christian History, The Principle Approach". San Francisco Foundation for American Christian Education. 1980.

Steinberg, B.S. "Indira Gandhi: The Relationship between Personality Profile and Leadership Style". International Society of Political Psychology. 2005.

Shamas–ur–RehmanToor& George Ofori. "Leadership versus Management: How They are Different, and Why". Online Journal. April 2008.

Sanders, Oswald J. Spiritual Leadership. Chicago : Moody Press, 1967.

The Holy Bible, King James Version.

Thompson, P.M. "The Stunted Vocation: An analysis of Jack Welch's Vision of Business Leadership". 2004.

The American Heritage Dictionary of Business Terms. Harcourt Publishing Company. 2010.

Tambo, O. R. "Nelson Mandela". No easy walk to freedom: Articles, speeches, and trial addresses, edited by Ruth First. New York: Basic Books. 1965.

Vitz, Paul C. " Family Decline: The findings of Social Science". Catholic Education Resource Centre. December 28, 2010.

Wilkes , Gene C. Jesus on Leadership: Becoming a Servant Leader. Life way Press. USA. 1996.

Walker , Paul. The Ministry of Church and Pastor. Pathway Press. 1965

Walumbwa, F., Avolio, B., Gardner, W. Wernsing,T. , Peterson, S. "Authentic Leadership : Development and Validation of a Theory Based Measure". Management Department. 2008

Warren Wiersbe. "Principles are the Bottom Line".
  http://management.about.com/od/leadership/a/FromMgr2L dr05.htm 1980.

CPSIA information can be obtained at www.ICGtesting.com
Printed in the USA
BVOW07s1435220114

342704BV00001B/12/P